More Than One

More Than One

PLURAL MARRIAGE

A SACRED HERITAGE
A PROMISE FOR TOMORROW

Shane LeGrande Whelan

ZION PUBLISHERS
Bountiful, Utah

Cover Artwork by Lester B. Lee

More Than One
Copyright © 2001 by Shane LeGrande Whelan
All rights reserved. Printed in the United States of America.

No part of this book may be used or reproduced in any manner whatsoever without written permission except in the case of brief quotations embodied in critical articles and reviews. This book is not an official publication of the Church of Jesus Christ of Latter-day Saints. The views expressed herein are the sole responsibility of the author and do not necessarily reflect the position of the Church of Jesus Christ of Latter-day Saints, Zion Publishers, or any other entity.

First Printing: November 2001
Second Printing: (Revised) February 2002

Library of Congress Cataloging-in-Publication Data has been applied for.
ISBN: 0-9717704-2-5 (previously ISBN: 1-57636-128-4)

If you would like to contact the author or if you have pioneer stories, journal entries or photos that you would like to have considered for the next printing of *More Than One*, write to Zion Publishers, P.O. Box 1382, Bountiful, Utah 84011, mto@zionpublishers.com or call 1-866-298-8811.

To order additional copies contact Zion Publishers or visit our website at
www.zionpublishers.com

Dedicated to my wife Rhonda, a true companion, whose faith in me and my ability to write this book was my real inspiration. Her patience, devotion and spiritual strength have been the greatest story of *More Than One*.

Contents

Preface viii

Part One…
A Sacred Heritage

Chapter One
    INTRODUCTION 1
Chapter Two
    THE REVELATION 7
Chapter Three
    MORE THAN ONE 27
Chapter Four
    THE JOYS & BLESSINGS 77
Chapter Five
    A RIGHTEOUS POSTERITY 113

Part Two…
A Promise for Tomorrow

Chapter Six
    A DIVINE PURPOSE 151
Chapter Seven
    NO MORE CHILDREN 163

Chapter Eight
SAVING THE FAMILY 179
Chapter Nine
RESTORING ALL THINGS 191
Chapter Ten
CONCLUSION 207

Appendix 215

Appendix A
DOCTRINE & COVENANTS, SECTION 132 215
Appendix B
THE RULES OF PLURAL MARRIAGE 225
Appendix C
THE FAMILY: A PROCLAMATION TO THE WORLD 243

End Notes 247

Index 257

Preface

I am an active member of the Church of Jesus Christ of Latter-day Saints, and like most church members, I had only a limited knowledge of polygamy and an incorrect perception of how this principle should be practiced. This understanding was changed, however, as I read more and more about my wife's family; great grandparents, both maternal and paternal, had lived plural marriage as members of the early Church.

As I began to research their stories and the history of Mormon plural marriage in general, I discovered many popular misconceptions that are held by church members and non-members alike. For decades books, movies and media have depicted this principle in a very negative light—as being a very shaded and problematic lifestyle. In their effort to tell the "true story," they have succeeded in bringing shame, ridicule and dishonor to a people who have sacrificed a great deal in order to keep a commandment of the Lord. In defense of these early Saints, I felt prompted to write this book about plural marriage—its purpose, joys and blessings.

As a result, hundreds of journals, diaries, stories and writings of those who once practiced this divine principle have been studied. In the process, I began to develop my own strong testimony of plural marriage. I believe it is a true and pure principle that will once again be practiced among the Saints as part of the restoration of the fullness of the gospel and in preparation of the Savior's Second Coming. Whether or not this will happen in my lifetime, I do not know, but it is a principle that has touched my spirit deeply.

~ the Author
November 2001

Part One

A Sacred Heritage

Chapter One

INTRODUCTION

It is estimated that during the late 1800's nearly 20 percent of the Church of Jesus Christ of Latter-day Saints practiced plural marriage or "polygamy," as it is often referred to. Although much has been written about the subject, little is known about the feelings, testimonies, and commitment of those individuals and families who accepted this divine calling and embraced it with true love and devotion.

Within our history lies a great heritage of wisdom and knowledge—a heritage left us by the Saints that first initiated the practice of plural marriage as restored by the Prophet Joseph Smith. Unfortunately, memories of these unique pioneers and their way of life, have faded with time. The majority of their words, like many truths, have been shuffled and buried under the concerns of today and are being hidden from view or destroyed by man in an effort to change the real history of these people.

But in the heritage they have left behind, we can find the truth, the love, and the priceless stories of those who lived this divine principle. This has been given to us as a gift, to hold in our hearts and cherish in our minds—the words of those who had the foresight to record their testimonies for future generations. For us it is an opportunity to better understand the joys and blessings of this noble work, as we listen to each brother, to each sister, and the voices of more than one as they speak to us from the past.

To raise my voice in public has ever been a source of much embarrassment to my sensitive nature, indeed I always feel my inability to address even my sisters in this capacity, but "duty and justice" demand that my voice should now be heard and would that my

words of faith in the defense of my religion might re-echo and find an accordance in the heart of every true-hearted woman throughout the length and breadth of our country.

Photo Courtesy of Daughters of Utah Pioneers

I know the principle of Plural Marriage to be a truth. I have lived in Polygamy for the last thirty-three years and was among the first to enter that sacred principle. I have shared hunger, poverty and toil with my husband's first wife whom I love as a dear sister; together we trod the trackless wilds to reach these then sterile valleys; together we battled the hardships of the "first year" the remembrance of those days are too indelibly stamped upon my mind ever to be erased; I have seen my husband stagger for want of food. I have heard my babies cry for bread and had nothing to give them; but with unceasing toil and by the blessings of God our efforts were crowned with success; how well I remember the first bread although made of course unbolted flour, it was "manna to our taste."

Through those trying scenes ties closer than those of sister-hood bound us together and the principle of Plural Marriage was firmly planted in our souls; and now that peaceful homes and smiling plenty have succeeded those bitter hardships these invaders come seeking to spread destruction through our fair Eden by sundering these sacred family ties, and may God mete out to them even the measure they are seeking to mete out to us.[1]

~ *Helen M. Callister*

Today we share the trust of our forefathers who gave us the responsibility to seek out the valuable truths in our history. We should not be blinded by those who profess to be true historians or scholars who would seek to destroy the foundation that so many have sacrificed so much to build. We should reject the words of those who attempt to sever our family ties, who want to bury a once sacred truth, and who endeavor to take away a heritage that is rightfully ours. The latter-day prophet and president of the Church of Jesus Christ of Latter-day Saints, Gordon B. Hinckley, has given this wise counsel:

> We must not be trapped by the sophistry of the world, which for the most part is negative and which seldom, if ever, bears good fruit. We must not be ensnared by or lean on the words of those clever ones whose self-appointed mission is to demean that which is sacred, to emphasize human weakness rather than inspired strength, and to undermine faith.[2]

It is our responsibility as children of our Father in Heaven to seek out those things of great worth, to build our lives and character upon the parts of our history that instill virtue, hope, and a promise for tomorrow. It is in the following chapters that we will find this truth, hope, and promise. It is here that we will find the "greatest love story ever told." It will not be the romantic story of a man and woman falling in love, nor the story of a loving couple struggling through life's difficulties and tragedies. It will not be anything commonplace or superficial, but rather the story of a great eternal love, shared by a particular group of courageous men and women who have embraced one of heaven's most divine principles. It is a story of sacrifice, devotion and love between eternal partners—a marriage of *more than one*.

Used by permission, Utah State Historical Society, all rights reserved.

Chapter Two

THE REVELATION

"It matterth not whether the principle is popular or unpopular, I will always maintain a true principle even if I stand alone in it."[1]
~ *Joseph Smith*

In a small brick store near the banks of the Mississippi River, Joseph Smith, founder of the Church of Jesus Christ of Latter-day Saints, dictated the revelation on plural marriage to his personal secretary and scribe, William Clayton. It was here in Nauvoo, Illinois, in the year 1843, that the Prophet Joseph Smith first committed to writing the revelation from the Lord concerning plural marriage.

Although there have been many published accounts of this revelation, one of the most compelling is found in a letter written by William Clayton in November of 1871. Responding to an inquiry about the Prophet Joseph Smith and the revelation on celestial marriage, William described the circumstances surrounding the revelation, adding his sincere and convincing testimony of plural marriage.

8 ~ *More Than One...*

Salt Lake City, Nov. 11, 1871.
Madison M. Scott Est.

Dear Sir;

Your letter of 23 June last was received by due course of mail, but owing to my being so very closely confined with public duties which has almost destroyed my health, I have not answered your letter so promptly as is my practice. My health is yet very poor, but I have resigned the office which was bearing so heavy upon me, and am in hopes to regain my usual sound health.

Now in regard to the subject matter of your letter, it appears to me the principle topic is what is commonly called polygamy, but which I prefer to call Celestial Marriage.

…Now I say to you as I am ready to testify to all the world and on which testimony I am most willing to meet all the Latter Day Saints and all apostates in time and through all eternity. I did write the Revelation on Celestial Marriage given through the Prophet Joseph Smith on the twelve day of July 1843. When the Revelation was written there was no one present except the prophet Joseph, his brother Hyrum and myself. It was written in the small office upstairs in the rear of the brick store which stood on the bank of the Mississippi River. It took some three hours to write it. Joseph dictated sentence by sentence and I wrote it as he dictated. After the whole was written Joseph requested me to read it slowly and carefully which I did, and he then pronounced it correct. The same night a copy was taken by Bishop

Used by permission, Utah State Historical Society; all rights reserved.

Whitney, which copy is now here, and which I know and testify is correct. The original was destroyed by Emma Smith.

I again testify that the revelation on Polygamy was given through the Prophet Joseph on the 12th July 1843, and that the Prophet Joseph both taught and practiced Polygamy I do positively know, and bear testimony to the fact.…I had the honor to seal one woman to Joseph under his direction. I could name ten or a dozen of his wives who are living now in this Territory, so that for any man to tell me that Joseph did not teach Polygamy he is losing his time, for I <u>know</u> better. It is not hearsay nor opinion with me, for I positively know of what I speak and I testify to the truth, and shall be willing to meet all opponents on the subject through all eternity. Anyone that says to the contrary does not know Joseph nor the mission the Lord gave him to fulfill.

Polygamy is a celestial order, the most sacred and holy that was ever revealed from Heaven to man. The revelation of July 12, 1843 says plainly, "To whomsoever this law is revealed they must and shall obey the same, or they shall be damned saith the Lord God." How any man who pretends to believe the Bible can fight against polygamy, is a mystery to me. Abraham and Jacob were Polygamists. One is called the "father of the faithful." Of the other it is said, *"In thee and in thy seed shall all the nations of the earth be blessed;"* so that there can be no blessings for the human family only through a Polygamist. I do not know where I could get a copy of the revelation or I would send you one. You may rest assured that no man that fights against Polygamy will have the privilege of sitting down with Abraham, Isaac and Jacob in the Kingdom of Heaven. I must close now. I could say much on this subject did time allow.…

Truly yours,
Wm. Clayton[2]

It is supposed that Joseph, in his study of the Bible in 1831, had questions concerning scriptures stating that Abraham, Isaac, and Jacob and other prophets of the Old Testament had many wives and concubines. This practice, approved of God, came into direct conflict with the religious teachings of the day, *i.e.*, that a man should have only one wife. Joseph sought clarification from the Lord regarding these scriptures and soon received enlightenment on the subject. *"Behold, and lo, I am the Lord thy God, and will answer thee as touching this matter"*[3] *(D&C 132:2).*

Through revelation, Joseph determined that when God commands it, as He did in ancient times, plural marriage is not sinful but a fulfillment of the Lord's plan. He further revealed to Joseph that the time had come to restore this divine principle, and commanded him as follows: *"Therefore, prepare thy heart to receive and obey the instructions which I am about to give unto you; for all those who have this law revealed unto them must obey the same"* (D&C 132:3). Although the Prophet was instructed in the principle and practiced it himself as early as 1833, it was not until 1843 that selected members of the Church received a written directive from the Lord restoring the practice of plural marriage.

The revelation later became part of the basic scriptures of the Church of Jesus Christ of Latter-day Saints as found in the Doctrine & Covenants, Section 132 (See Appendix A). It covers various aspects of the eternal order of families, as well as the promise of eternal increase and exaltation made to those who keep this "new and everlasting covenant." The revelation also discusses the relationship the Lord had with many of the Old Testament prophets and how their participation in plural marriage was not only a common practice, but a commandment given to further the kingdom of God here upon the earth.

Abraham, one of these prophets, not only practiced plural marriage, but was assured of exaltation from the Lord. In verse 29 of the 132nd section it states the following: *"Abraham received all things, whatsoever he received, by revelation and commandment, by my word, saith the Lord, and hath entered into his exaltation and sitteth upon his throne."* This part of the revelation goes on to explain that Abraham received certain promises concerning his seed—one being that his seed would continue in this world, and second that his seed would continue into the eternities. Last and most important is the promise the Lord gave Abraham that in both this world and the next, his seed would be as innumerable as the stars and as countless as the sand on the seashore.

> Abraham received promises concerning his seed, and of the fruit of his loins—from whose loins ye are, namely, my servant Joseph—which were to continue so long as they were in the world; and as touching Abraham and his seed, out of the world they should continue; both in the world and out of the world should they continue as innumerable as the stars; or, if ye were to count the sand upon the seashore ye could not number them (D&C 132:30).

One of the most notable parts of the revelation is the promise given to Joseph that he would share in the blessings of Abraham. This promise was contingent upon his obedience to the following verse, wherein it directs Joseph to go and *"do the works of Abraham"* by entering into the law of plural marriage.

> This promise is yours also, because ye are of Abraham, and the promise was made unto Abraham; and by this law is the continuation of the works of my Father, wherein he glorifieth himself. Go ye,

therefore, and do the works of Abraham; enter ye into my law and ye shall be saved. But if ye enter not into my law ye cannot receive the promise of my Father, which he made unto Abraham (D&C 132: 31-33).

Joseph complied with the Lord's command and later began instructing those closest to him on the aspects of plural marriage. The prophet's wife, Emma, was one of the first to read the revelation. Her initial response of disapproval led to the destruction of the original copy as she struggled with the thought of sharing her husband with other wives. Her life would be filled with anguish and heartache, as well as feelings of joy and sisterhood, as she began to acknowledge the other wives in Joseph's life. Although many have written about Emma's displeasure in her husband's obedience to the "principle," it has been documented that Emma did at times strive to accept and even administer it according to the Lord's direction. In a response to a newspaper article about Emma, one of Joseph's wives, Eliza R. Snow, who had lived in the Smith home, stated the following:

> It is a fact that Sister Emma, of her own free will and choice, gave her husband four wives, two of whom are now living, and ready to testify that she, not only gave them to her husband, but that she taught them the doctrine of plural marriage and urged them to accept it.[4]

Emily Partridge, one of the wives given to Joseph by Emma, would later write, *"I know it was hard for Emma, and any woman to enter plural marriage in those days,…I do not know as anybody would have done any better than Emma did under the circumstance."*[5] Although it was very difficult for Emma, the desire to support her husband in his prophetic calling is evident in a personal blessing she requested from Joseph, just prior to his martyrdom. Unable to be with Emma, he instructed her to write those things that she desired most and he would sign the blessing. Among the many sincere requests of her heart, Emma listed as one of the last and most important, the desire to honor and sustain her husband and to act in unison with all that he did. She penned the following for Joseph's signature:

These desires of my heart were called forth by Joseph sending me word...that he had not time to write as he would like, but I could write out the best blessing I could think of and he would sign the same on his return.

First of all I would crave as the richest of heaven's blessings would be wisdom from my Heavenly Father bestowed daily, so that what ever I do or say, I could not look back at the close of the day with regret, nor neglect the performance of any act that would bring a blessing. I desire the Spirit of God to know and understand myself, I desire a fruitful, active mind, that I may be able to comprehend the designs of God, when revealed through his servants without doubting. I desire the spirit of discernment, which is one of the promised blessings of the Holy Ghost.

I particularly desire wisdom to bring up all children that are, or may be committed to my charge, in any manner that they will be useful ornaments in the Kingdom of God, and in a coming day arise up and call me blessed. I desire prudence that I may not through ambition abuse my body and cause it to become old and care-worn, but that I may wear a cheerful countenance, living to perform all the work that I covenanted to perform in the spirit-world and be a blessing to all who may need aught at my hands.

I desire with all my heart to honor and respect my husband as my head, ever to live in his confidence and by acting in unison with him retain the place which God has given me by his side, and I ask my Heavenly Father, that through humility, I may be enabled to overcome the curse which was pronounced on the daughters of Eve. I desire to see that I may rejoice with them in the blessings which God has in store for all who are willing to be obedient to his requirements. Finally, I desire that whatever may be my lot through life I may be enabled to acknowledge the hand of God in all things.[6]

Although the marriage she had hoped for was cut short by the martyrdom of her husband, she had shared a significant portion of her life with a prophet of God. Her life had been forever changed; but when the Saints made their exodus west, Emma remained. At her home in Nauvoo, Emma, at the age of 74, passed from this life to the next to the waiting arms of her loving husband. With her last breath, her arm out stretched, she called her husband by name, "*Joseph! Joseph! Joseph!*"[7] As the first wife in this dispensation to participate in plural marriage, Emma stands as an example of courage and compassion, as she struggled to overcome the feelings of jealousy, doubt, and fear.

In addition to Emma, there were many others who received confirmation through personal revelation that this principle was true, and that it was indeed from a loving Heavenly Father who desired to bless his children. One of these individuals, Lucy Walker, at age 16, was approached by Joseph Smith, asking her to become his wife. She later shared her testimony:

> In the year 1842 President Joseph Smith sought an interview with me and said, "I have a message for you. I have been commanded of God to take another wife and you are the woman." My astonishment knew no bounds. This announcement was indeed a thunderbolt to me. He asked me if I believed him to be a prophet of God "Most assuredly I do," I replied. He fully explained to me the principle of Plural or Celestial Marriage. He said this principle was again to be restored for the benefit of the human family, that it would prove an everlasting blessing to my father's house and form a chain that could never be broken, worlds without end. "What have you to say" he asked. "Nothing." How could I speak or what could I say? He said "If you will pray sincerely for light and understanding in relation thereto, you shall receive a testimony of the correctness of this principle." I felt I prayed sincerely but was so unwilling to consider the matter favorable that I fear I did not ask in faith or light. Gross Darkness instead of light took possession of my mind. I was tempted and tortured beyond endurance until life was not desirable. Oh that the grave would kindly receive me, that I might find rest on the bosom of my dear mother. Why should I be chosen from among thy daughters, Father, I am only a child in years and experience. No mother to counsel; no father near to tell

Courtesy of LDS Church Historical Department

what to do in this trying hour. Oh, let this bitter cup pass. And thus I prayed in the agony of my soul.

The prophet discerned my sorrow. He saw how unhappy I was and sought an opportunity of again speaking to me on this subject and said, "Although I cannot under existing circumstances acknowledge you as my wife, the time is near when we will go beyond the Rocky Mountains and then you will be acknowledged and honored as my wife." He also said, "This principle will yet be believed in and practiced by the righteous. I have no flattering words to offer. It is a command of God to you. I will give you until tomorrow to decide this matter. If you reject this message the gate will be closed forever against you."

This aroused every drop of Scotch in my veins, for a few moments I stood fearless before him and looked him in the eye. I felt at this moment that I was called to place myself on the alter a living sacrifice—perhaps to brook the world in disgrace and incur the displeasure and contempt of my evil companions; all my dreams of happiness blown to the four winds. This was too much for as yet no shadow had crossed my path aside from the death of my dear mother. The future to me had been a bright, cloudless day. I had been speechless but at last found utterance and said, "Although you are a prophet of God you could not induce me to take a step of so great importance unless I know that God approves my course. I would rather die. I have tried to pray but received no comfort, no light." And emphatically forbid him speaking again to me on this subject. "Every feeling of my soul revolted against it" said I "the same God who has sent this message is the being I have worshipped from my early childhood and He must manifest His will to me." He walked across the room, returned and stood before me with the most beautiful expression of countenance and said, "God almighty loves you. You shall have a manifestation of the will of God concerning you, a testimony that you can never deny. I will tell you what it shall be. It shall be that joy and peace that you never knew."

Oh, how earnestly I prayed for these words to be fulfilled. It was near dawn after another sleepless night when my room was lighted up by a heavenly influence. To me it was, in comparison, like the brilliant sun bursting through the darkest cloud. My soul was filled with a calm sweet peace that "I never knew." Supreme happiness took possession of me and I received a powerful and irresistible testimony of the truth of Plural Marriage, which has been like an anchor to the soul through all the trials of life. I felt that I must go out into the morning air and give vent to the joy and gratitude that filled my soul. As I descended the stairs, President Smith opened the door below, took me by the hand and said, "Thank God, you have the testimony. I too have prayed." He led me to a chair, placed his hands upon my head and blessed me with every blessing my heart could possibly desire. The first day of May, 1843, I consented to become the Prophet's wife, and was sealed to him for time and all eternity at his own house by Elder William Clayton.

Today I have but one regret which is that I have not been a more worthy representative of the principle of Plural Marriage, and that I have not lived a more perfect life. I can also state that Emma Smith was present and did consent to Eliza and Emily Partridge, also Maria and Sara Lawrence being sealed to her husband. This I had from the prophet's own mouth, also the testimony of her niece, Hyrum Smith's eldest daughter (my brother Lorin's wife), as well as that of the young ladies named, themselves with whom I was on most intimate terms and was glad that they, too, had accepted that order of marriage. Instead of a feeling of jealousy it was a source of comfort to me. We were as sisters to each other.

> In this I acted in accordance with the will of God. Not for any worldly aggrandizement, not for the gratification of the flesh. How can it be said that we accepted this principle for any lustful desires? Preposterous. This would be utterly impossible but, as I said before, we accepted it to obey a command of God, to establish a principle that would benefit the human family and emancipate them from the degradation into which they had fallen through their wicked customs.
>
> In all this God had a road marked out for me that I knew not; to struggle against the tide of opposition, prejudice and tradition, to aid in establishing a principle that would exalt mankind and bring them back into his presence. A tie has been formed that will guide me to the highest and most glorious destiny, if I continue to walk in the regeneration, which is the grand object of my life.[8]

Many of those closest to the Prophet would receive similar confirmations, while numerous others would come to the knowledge that they, too, would play an effectual role in bringing forth the restoration of plural marriage. This knowledge would come by the shared testimony of others, divine instruction, or through dreams and visions. Whichever way the spirit was brought to bear upon these worthy saints, it was extended to both male and female, in all locales where the membership of the Church was being organized. In the words of Eliza R. Snow, we can find one of many such experiences, giving a clear view of the importance of plural marriage and the power by which it was brought forth.

> While my brother was absent on this, his first mission to Europe, changes had taken place with me, one of eternal import, of which I supposed him to be entirely ignorant. The Prophet Joseph had taught

me the principle of plural, or celestial marriage, and I was married to him for time and eternity. In consequence of the ignorance of most of the Saints, as well as people of the world, on this subject, it was not mentioned only privately between the few whose minds were enlightened on the subject.

…Not knowing how my brother would receive it, I did not feel at liberty, and did not wish to assume the responsibility of instructing him in the principle of plural marriage, and either maintained silence, or, to his indirect questioning, gave evasive answers, until I was forced, by his cool and distant manner, to feel that he was growing jealous of my sisterly confidence—that I could not confide in his brotherly integrity. I could not endure this—something must be done.

I informed my husband of the situation, and requested him to open the subject to my brother. A favorable opportunity soon presented, and, seated together on the lone bank of the Mississippi River, they had a most interesting conversation. The Prophet afterwards told me that he found that my brother's mind had been previously enlightened on the subject in question, and was ready to receive whatever the spirit of revelation from God should impart. That Comforter which Jesus said should "lead into all truth," had penetrated his understanding, and while in England had

Eliza's brother, Lorenzo Snow.

given him an intimation of what at that time was, to many, a secret. This was the result of living near the Lord, and holding communion with Him.[9]

Even with the spirit of the Lord touching so many hearts, it was not easy for the members of the Church to accept a concept so foreign to their upbringing. Their traditions and beliefs were so deeply imbedded that it was necessary for the Prophet and others to initiate this principle with secrecy. Also of great concern was the prevailing atmosphere of hatred and animosity toward the Saints by outsiders. This warranted yet further consideration by the Church as to what activities were made public. Not only was there conflict from without the Church, but also from within, as some Church leaders began to express their misgivings about plural marriage. Certainly the Prophet was not excluded from having his own difficulty with the principle. In the personal journal of Samuel Claridge, we find an insight to the Prophet's feelings as he spoke to a close friend:

> I remember at one time, talking to a brother by the name of Benjamin Johnson who was a confidential friend of Joseph Smith, and he said Joseph came to him one day when he was working and said to him, "I'm in trouble." He then told him that the Lord had commanded him to take another wife on the same principle as the Lord commanded Father Abraham, and he said, "I've put it off, and put it off, knowing it would come to contact with the feelings of the people and the great trial of their faith it would be, but just recently an angel of the Lord stood before me with a drawn sword in his hand and said if Joseph Smith did not go forth and obey that commandment, he would be cut off, and another one put in his place." Well, under these conditions, he went forth saying he would do the best he could, and

when he mentioned it to Brigham Young, Brigham made the reply, "Joseph, if you could excuse me, I would rather take my valise on my back and go and preach the gospel the remainder of my days."[10]

It was soon after this particular visitation from a heavenly messenger that Joseph embraced the principle, and in so doing fulfilled another requirement in the restoration of the gospel. It was Joseph's understanding that the Lord intended to restore all things in this dispensation that had been an essential part of past dispensations. As part of the revelation on celestial marriage, he told the Prophet the following; *"I am the Lord thy God, and I gave unto thee, my servant Joseph, an appointment, and restore all things"* (D&C 132:40). The keys of the priesthood, baptism for the living as well as the dead, along with plural marriage, were each important in this restoration of all things.

Following the Prophet's example and admonishment, other Church leaders slowly began to accept the principle, but not without much concern and trepidation. Many of the twelve apostles, who were some of the first brethren to become aware of the Lord's commandment, initially sought to oppose Joseph Smith in what they believed to be unacceptable doctrine. However, they later became staunch advocates of plural marriage and in most cases, embraced the practice themselves. Writing about this particular time in Church history, the author B.H. Roberts, in his *Comprehensive History of the Church*, observed the following:

> The world never made a greater mistake than when it supposed that plural marriage was hailed with delight by the elders who were commanded of the Lord to introduce its practice in this generation. They saw clearly that it would bring additional reproach upon them

from the world; that it would run counter to the traditions and prejudices of society, as, indeed, it was contrary to their own traditions; that their motives would be misunderstood or misconstrued. All this they saw, and naturally shrunk from the undertaking required of them by this doctrine.[11]

It was a time of great consequence, but with determination and a renewed faith in the Prophet, the leaders of the Church moved forward in the acceptance and practice of plural marriage. The Saints soon followed, learning line upon line, precept upon precept, as Joseph's teachings took hold throughout the Church. At every opportunity he instructed those he associated with, in particular his close friends. He spoke of the responsibilities, rewards, and consequences, as he understood them, having received his knowledge of the doctrine through divine revelation. His testimony of the restored gospel, as well as the eternal blessings for those who would enter into plural marriage, were expressed not only in his words, but in his very being.

One devoted sister, Mary Isabella Horne, gives her recollection of the Prophet's visit to the members in Canada. While staying at her family's home for several weeks, the Prophet gave his counsel and instruction to the saints in the area. She recalls that Joseph *"took pleasure in answering questions pertaining to the gospel and the organization of the church."*[12] Sharing those things that were sacred and true, he gave many people the opportunity to partake of his knowledge and testimony, thus reflecting his divine mission and calling.

> Having been requested by the late Apostle, Abraham Owen Woodruff, some months prior to his death, to leave my personal testimony to my children concerning the life, character, labors, and

mission of the Prophet Joseph Smith, as well as the divinity of the covenant of Plural Marriage, I cheerfully comply, as follows:

I first met the Prophet Joseph Smith in the fall of 1837, at my home in the town of Scarborough, Canada West. When I first shook hands with him I was thrilled through and through, and I knew that he was a Prophet of God, and that testimony has never left me, but is still strong within me, and has been a monitor to me, so that I can now bear a faithful testimony to the divinity of the mission of that Great Man of God.

…I testify that Joseph Smith was the greatest Prophet that ever lived on this earth, the Savior, only, accepted. There was a personal magnetism about him which drew all people who became acquainted with him, to him.

I feel greatly honored when I realize that I have had the privilege of personally entertaining this great man, administrating to his temporal wants, of shaking hands with him, and listening to his voice. I heard him relate his first vision when the Father and Son appeared to him; also his receiving the Gold Plates from the angel Moroni. This recital was given in compliance with a special request of a few particular friends in the home of Sister Walton, whose house was ever open to the saints. While he was relating the circumstances, the Prophet's countenance lighted up, a full and wonderful a power accompanied his words that everybody who heard them felt his influence and power, and no one could doubt the truth of his narration.

Photo used by permission, Utah State Historical Society, all rights reserved.

> I know that he was true to his trust, and that the Principles that he addressed and taught are true. I solemnly testify that I know that the Principle of Plural Marriage is true; that it came direct from God; I have had evidence of it's truthfulness, and have lived in it for nearly fifty years. I counsel all my posterity to avoid condemning or making light of this sacred principle.[13]
>
> ~ *Mary Isabella Horne ~ first wife of Joseph Horne*

Through the efforts of Joseph Smith and other Church leaders, the principle of plural marriage began to spread throughout the Church. For many of the men and women it was a time of great trial as they considered their obedience to this "new and everlasting covenant of marriage" or plurality of wives. Although there was great difficulty in accepting the principle, it moved forward, as does all God's work. Even after the martyrdom of the Prophet in 1844, the principle remained firmly established within many families of the Church and continued to increase in acceptance.

From the banks of the Mississippi to the shores of the Great Salt Lake, the principle followed the migration of the Saints. As they began to establish their new Zion, the newly called prophet and leader of the Church, Brigham Young, rose up and professed its divine importance, inviting all to accept the principle and enjoy the eternal blessings that would follow. He extended a personal invitation to numerous families and individuals to participate in plural marriage, making not only family resources, but emotional resources available to the thousands of converts arriving in the Salt Lake Valley, many of whom were single sisters and widowed mothers.

President Young continued to embrace the principle with great enthusiasm and instructed Elder Orson Pratt to formally announce the "revelation of plural marriage" to the body of the Church during a special two-day conference held August 29, 1852, in Salt Lake City. From this announcement came a public awareness that the Church had now made plural marriage an official doctrine and practice.

Elder Pratt was further instructed to travel to Washington, D.C., and establish an office for the primary purpose of proclaiming and defending the basic principles of the Church, in particular the principle of plural marriage, to the nation and its leaders. Thus Pratt began printing numerous articles regarding celestial marriage in a monthly publication called "*The Seer*," providing one of the most convincing defenses of plural marriage on record. From the beginnings of plural marriage in Old Testament times to the sanction of the practice by reformers such as Martin Luther, the presentation of facts and logic by Orson Pratt, along with his knowledge of theology, was unprecedented. Of particular interest were the rules of plural marriage (See Appendix B), 27 items that should be followed by families in the Church who were living the principle. This became an inspired guideline for the Saints in the years that followed.

The efforts of Orson Pratt as well as many others who were sent abroad to proclaim and defend plural marriage brought an increasing awareness that the gospel, including plural marriage, had been restored as foretold by the prophets of old. The sisters at home proclaimed their beliefs as well. Women of great influence such as Emmeline Wells, Eliza R. Snow, and Helen Mar Whitney, used their exceptional skills in writing and speaking to defend the great concourse of sisters participating in the principle.

In the years that followed, women such as Elizabeth J. Roundy and Wilmarth East visited 54 settlements throughout the state in an effort to obtain support for women's rights. As a result of their labors, a petition signed by over 26,000 women was presented in December 1875 to the Congress of the United States declaring their allegiance to the Constitution and demanding their rights as American citizens, as well as proclaiming their belief in God and the divine practice of plural marriage.[14]

These women who supported plural marriage and opposed those who were making every effort to outlaw its practice, continued to hold mass meetings throughout the state. Over 1,500 women attended one such meeting held in Salt Lake City on November 16, 1878, giving a clear message to the gentiles that plural marriage was an essential part of their life, and they were prepared to defend it at all costs.

President Brigham Young offered this observation, *"Plural marriage will be fostered and believed in by the more intelligent portion of the world as one of the best doctrines ever proclaimed to any people...."*[15] Whether he was referring to his own time or prophesying of some future time is unsure. In either case, the impact of Joseph's revelation left no question that families living the principle would become a dominant force.

By the late 1800's participation in plural marriage involved nearly twenty percent of the church membership. It was this group of obedient and faithful Saints, who laid their hearts on the line and made the sacrifice, who would prove to be a blessing of eternal consequence—a blessing to *more than one.*

Photo used by permission, Utah State Historical Society, all rights reserved.

Chapter Three

MORE THAN ONE

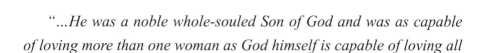

"...He was a noble whole-souled Son of God and was as capable of loving more than one woman as God himself is capable of loving all his creations."[1]

~ Lucy Walker Kimball

In the early days of the Church there were many men and women who came to a realization that their destiny lay within the bounds of plural marriage. This came by personal revelation through dreams, spiritual promptings and destined meetings. Even before the revelation on plural marriage was given, there were individuals who came to the knowledge that this principle was ordained of God and would be brought back as part of the restoration of all things. Many received a testimony of Joseph Smith and other Church leaders who practiced and taught plural marriage. This was all in preparation for the change that would soon come into their lives—a change that would not only bring a fulfillment of promises, but also secure blessings for generations to come.

The following testimonies, journal entries and recollections bear witness to the eternal principle of plural marriage and its divine

Martin Benjamin Bushman

We was married on the twenty second of March, 1868 by Brigham Young. We stayed with her parents one week then moved to our home. One year later we had a baby girl born to us but she only lived sixteen days when she died. One year later we had twins born to us, a boy and a girl. They both lived so we had to get a girl to help us to take care of them.

We obtained the service of a young lady by the name of Martha Weslton. She lived with us for two years. We got so attached to her that I asked her if she would marry me as a plural wife. She said she would if her parents would give their consent. It was then that I realized the responsibility that I was taken upon myself, being a young man only twenty-six years old and poor circumstances to take care of two families.

So I went to the Lord in secret prayer and asked that if it was his will that I should marry her that it would be so. If not, may some thing turn up to stop the marriage. I had learned by reading the revelation on that subject that man may marry more than one wife. If he chooses it for a righteous purpose, it would be attended with blessings and after living in that order for forty years, I have been blessed with means and provided homes for my children and have had joy in doing so. Those were the best days of my life.

Her parents and my wife freely gave their consent and was married on the second of March 1867 by Wilford Woodruff. Both the wives and the children lived in peace in the same house for ten years. Then I provided each with a home and have not had to call on any to help me out of debt.

…I made it a practice to live with each family the same that I might help them with their children and have prayers with them. I tried to set a good example before my children by having prayers night and morning and going to Sunday School and to meetings, also by paying tithing and all other requirements.

I wish to say that my wives and children have tried to obey my council and showed me all the respect that I could ask of them.[2]

Samuel Claridge

I put it to myself—how would I feel if I was a boy, to see my father bring another wife to the family? I should naturally rebel, notwithstanding I was taught by my mother that the Bible was the word of God, and that Abraham and others were amongst the best men that ever lived, and the special favored of heaven, but I'll skip over all that.…

Under these conditions I took a plural wife and one asked—"Did you not have difficulty?" Oh yes, the greatest I ever had in my life, and when the great day of reckoning comes, and the books are opened, and you see what my women passed through to keep the commandments of the Lord, you would never more persecute the polygamists, but the Lord said that those that enter into this with a pure motive, they should be visited with blessings, and they should have a testimony to the truth of the principle.

Fortunately for me, I had one of the most patient, noble-hearted wives who knew this was the work of the Lord, and under a conscientious sense of her duty, she consented for me to take another wife, and has acted a noble part in helping me to carry it out, but was it not a trial to her? Oh, indeed, and she shed many a bitter tear but she prayed to her Heavenly Father to give her strength to over come, and her prayers were answered, and she was a mother to my second wife and her children and gained a victory over herself—gone to her eternal rest some twenty-five years ago.[3]

Helen Mar Whitney ~ daughter of Heber C. & Vilate Kimball

My mother told me repeatedly that she could not doubt that this plural order was of divine origin, for the Lord has shown it to her in answer to prayer. She was so conscientious and of such strong faith, that she never doubted after once being convinced of the truth, but she had to be convinced before accepting any principle. It was three weeks after my father was baptized into this Church before she could see the necessity of again submitting to that ordinance, as they had both been baptized into the Baptist church a short time previous to hearing "Mormonism." During that period my father mourned for her as one would mourn for the dead; but he prayed unceasingly that she might see and accept the truth. In Nauvoo my father, among others of his brethren, was taught the plural wife doctrine and he was told by Joseph Smith, the prophet, three times to go and take a certain woman; but not till he had commanded him in the name of the Lord did he obey. At the same time Joseph told him not to divulge this secret, not even to my mother, for fear that she would not receive it, for his life was in constant jeopardy, not only from outside influences and enemies, who were seeking some plea to take him back into Missouri, but from false brethren who had crept like snakes into his bosom and then betrayed him. There were also treacherous women who were double-tongued and went about doing all the mischief that was possible.

My father realized the situation fully, and the love and reverence he bore for the Prophet were so great that he would sooner have laid down his own life than have betrayed him. This was the greatest test of his faith that he had ever experienced. When first hearing the principle taught, believing that he would be required to enter this order, he thought of two elderly sisters who were great friends of my mother, and who he believed would cause her little if any unhappiness. The woman he was told to take, however, was an English lady, nearer my mother's age, who came over with her husband and two little girls with a company of Saints, in the same ship in which President B. Young and my father returned from their second mission to Europe. She had been reared in luxury but was unfortunate in marriage. Though her husband was of respectable and wealthy parents, and capable of carrying on a large business, he was a very dissipated man and ran through his own means and all of hers that he could obtain. She had three wealthy brothers, who took charge of her property to prevent her husband from squandering it. He loved her and their little daughters with all the affection of which he was capable, but was so brutal to them when under the influence of drink that she twice had been obligated to leave him and seek refuge in the homes of her brothers. But after many professions and promises of reform, she was induced each time to return.

Upon hearing the gospel she received it, as also her husband, but he had not sufficient religion to control his appetite. Her brothers considered this step unpardonable, and thought they were more disgraced by her joining the awful people called "Mormons," than in living with a drunken and dissolute husband. The first time I saw him was a few days after their arrival in Nauvoo; he was then half intoxicated. She was of a proud and sensitive nature, and being among strangers in a strange land, it placed her under peculiar and very trying circumstances.

My father and mother and the neighbors were very kind to her, and she was assisted in finding a house to rent, which belonged to an old settler in Commerce. While living there the husband came home so drunk that his abusive treatment of his wife and children outraged the feelings of Mr. Hibbard and family, and they interfered and drove him from the premises. She could no longer live with him, and he soon afterwards returned to England.

It was somewhere near this time that my father was commanded to take her and her children and provide for them. But the thought of deceiving the kind and faithful wife of his youth, whom he loved with all his heart, and who with him had borne so patiently their separations and all the trials and sacrifices they had been called to endure, was more than he felt able to bear. He realized not only the addition of trouble and perplexities that such a step would bring upon him (and in those days nearly all his time was spent in the Lord's vineyard), but his sorrow and misery were increased by the thought of her delicate condition, as well as fearing that she might hear it from some other source, which would no doubt separate them forever, and he shrank from the thought of doing anything to cause her unhappiness.

Finally he came to the conclusion to tell Joseph how he felt, and he did so, telling him he was fearful that if he took this step the trial would be greater than he could bear, and it might induce him to do that which would cause him to forfeit his salvation. The Prophet had loved him from the time they first met each other in Kirtland, and he felt such sympathy for him that he went and inquired of the Lord; His answer was: "Tell him to go and do as he has been commanded, and if I see that there is any danger of his apostatizing I will take him to myself." This shows that the trial must have been extraordinary, for he was a man who, from the first, had yielded implicit obedience to every requirement of the Prophet.

My mother had noticed a change in his manner and appearance, and when she inquired the cause he tried to evade her questions, saying it was only her imagination or he was not feeling well, etc. But at last he promised he would tell her after a while, if she would only wait. This trouble so worked upon his mind that his anxious and haggard looks betrayed him daily and hourly, and finally his misery became so unbearable that it was impossible to control his feelings. He became sick in body, but his mental wretchedness was too great to allow of his retiring and he would walk the floor till nearly morning, and sometimes the agony of his mind was so terrible that he would wring his hands and weep like a child, and beseech the Lord to be merciful and reveal to her this celestial principle, for he himself could not break his vow of secrecy.

The anguish of their hearts was indescribable, and when she found it was useless to beseech him longer she retired to her room and bowed before the Lord and poured out her soul in prayer to Him who hath said: "If any lack wisdom let him ask of God, who giveth to all men liberally and upbraideth not." "Seek and ye shall find, knock and it shall be opened unto you." My father's heart was raised at the same time in supplication, and while pleading as one would plead for life, the vision of her mind was opened, and as darkness flees before the morning sun, so did her sorrow and the groveling things of earth vanish away.

Before her was illustrated the order of celestial marriage, in all its beauty and glory, together with the great exaltation and honor it would confer upon her in that immortal and celestial sphere, if she would accept it and stand in her place by her husband's side. She also saw the woman he had taken to wife and contemplated with joy the vast and boundless love and union which this order would bring about, as well as the increase of her husband's kingdoms, and the power and glory extending throughout the eternities, worlds without end.

She related the scene to me and to many others and said her soul was satisfied, for she was filled with the Spirit of God. With a countenance beaming with joy she returned to my father, saying, "Heber, what you kept from me the Lord has shown to me." She told me she never saw so happy a man as father was when she described the vision and told him she was satisfied and knew that it was from God. She covenanted there and then to stand by him and honor the principle, which covenant she faithfully kept, and though her trials were often heavy and grievous to bear, she knew that father and his other wives were also being tried, and her integrity was unflinching to the end. He was heard repeatedly to say that he had shed rivers of tears over this order—the order of celestial or plural marriage.[4]

Christopher J. Arthur

Winter has come and with it, it's tithing labors, which took from my mind the ever ebbing thoughts too frequently engaged in when there is nothing to occupy our time and mind. Day and night my time is fully spent, either on my books or on attending meetings. During the late winter months Julia Pamelia Dury was my housekeeper, but most of the time the place was filled by A.E. [*Elizabeth*] Perry. Early in 1875 I dreamed seeing all the children kissing Elizabeth while Caroline looked on with holy favor. Again I saw Elizabeth and Pamelia represented by figures when it was manifested that Elizabeth should be mine and Pamelia was hidden. This satisfied me and I asked Bro. Perry for his daughter. He readily granted me my request. Then I asked Elizabeth, who consented.[5]

Elizabeth Acord Beck ~ second wife of Erastus Beck

My own father was a polygamist—had three wives—and I say this to you in all sincerity, I didn't see one thing in my father's household that made me dislike polygamy. I always believed in it, that it was a true principle, and through it and it alone could we obtain the greatest blessings and live as fully as we should. Yet believing this I found it hard to go into polygamy. My husband courted me for five years—and courtships weren't usually so long in those days. Oh, I went with other boys and men and considered marrying some of them. I often told Dad that the only reason I married him was because he pestered me so much. He used to take me out and while I thoroughly liked and respected him…he was a great friend of my father's. Father was always kind to people and he was always taking young boys under his wing. Dad had been close to him since he was a little fellow. In fact, when Father moved to Mexico Dad helped him do it. I wasn't engaged to him then either.

Well, after he had taken me out his wife came to me and told me that she believed in polygamy and that she wanted her husband to marry again and that she would like to have me be his second wife. She was a kind and lovely woman and I was happy that she felt that way. Still I could not make up my mind to marry him. Even when I promised him I was doubtful. He would come to see me and I would tell him that I couldn't. It was just before the Manifesto was issued that I finally promised him. People all over Utah were upset and harried and there was beginning to be different feeling about polygamy. I believed in it utterly but I wondered if I would be strong enough to live it. There were a number of fine men who wanted me to marry them and I couldn't decide. When I told Mother, who believed in it as I did, she could not make up her mind to it. She feared that I would not develop the qualities necessary to living it and she wanted me to be happy. One night she dreamed that she went to the Bible to find solace and perhaps an answer to whether I should marry Dad. She dreamed that she opened the Bible and her eyes fell on this passage, "If it were not so, why were ye comforted?" Then, still in her dream, she went back to bed, happy. After that she was convinced that it was the best thing to do. I did it and I have never regretted it. Perhaps I should not say that because there were times when I felt that I had more than I could bear and I became disgruntled. But those times happen to any wife in monogamy, and on the whole I was very happy.[6]

Miles Edgar Johnson

On the first day of September 1884 (Tuesday), Seymore B. Young of the First Council of Seventies came to Huntington to organize the 81st Quorum of Seventies. The Elders roll of which I was Secretary was inspected and my name was the first name called, of the twenty-one names selected…

On the Tuesday before when my name was called, my soul seemed to revolt against it for some reason, and the longer I had to think about it the more determined I was to refuse to be ordained a Seventy. I was very much afraid they would call on me to take a second wife; however, I kept this to myself but I moped around for four days. I was very miserable and upset.

I dared not tell my wife of my fears, as there had not been a word said on the subject at the meeting on Tuesday, and there was apparently no cause for my frustration. But I couldn't shake it off.…I silently slipped into the bedroom and threw myself across the bed thinking I was alone with my thoughts. I had been there but a moment with my face buried in my arms; when my dear wife came silently into the room and sat on the bed beside me patting me gently on the back, she said she knew what was troubling me. She said she had been watching me since last Tuesday…She said she loved me dearly, but thought she had married a man who would be willing to live any requirement or principle of the Gospel. She said she was proud of me when I was the first man chosen to be ordained a Seventy.

"I will now tell you that if you are afraid they will ask you to take another wife, I'm proud to tell you that I will live any principle of the Gospel that I am called to live. If you are not a coward you will go…"

By the time she had finished, I was on my feet. I felt like a whipped pup. I told her she had always been a better Latter-day Saint than I, and if she felt that way I would go at once.

When I had gone but a short way, I met Brother Samuel Grange, an older man than I, and a personal friend. He asked me what was bothering me. He said he had been sitting at home reading and he kept thinking about me, and he felt that I was having trouble and felt the urge to come and see me. While we were talking the other men came past on their way to the church house to be ordained and urged me to join them.

After listening to a talk on Celestial Marriage by Elder Young, he said we would be asked to make the Covenant to take other wives, as it would not be very long before the opportunity would be taken away. (This was about fourteen years before the Manifesto in 1890.) When he told us to stand if we would do as asked, we all stood and said we would. Of course, I felt this to be a sacred promise and fully intended to keep it, being aided by my dear wife. When I got home, we talked about it and it was mutually agreed that as soon as we saw a girl that suited us, and who was willing we would make that promise good.

On the 10th day of the same month (six days later), a plump little black eyed girl, with a beautiful supply of long black hair came into the Post Office and asked for mail. She was a stranger to both of us, and when she went out my wife said, "There's your girl." Later we were informed that she was the daughter of Samuel Rowley, Miss Hannah Eliza, who had just come into our town that day. She came often for mail and we got better acquainted. My wife and I talked about how well behaved and shy she was.

[*In November of 1885 his wife died a few days after giving birth prematurely to a daughter. The daughter only lived twelve hours and the mother for a few days after that. She died in the arms of Miles, expressing her love for him with her last breath. For the next two years, Miles grieved over the loss of his dear wife Alice but with the help of friends and family his life continued on. His journal further states:*]

As time passed some of the boys stopped at the store and encouraged me to go with them to choir practice, and in time the ice was broken and I attended the dances. One Sunday afternoon in April of 1887, I was alone and lonesome, so decided to visit my sister Julia. I filled my pockets with candy and nuts for the children. When I got outside I met William H. Leonard and he wanted me to go with him over to the church house where some girls gathered, waiting for the evening meeting. I told him I was on my way to visit my sister which was in the same direction. When we arrived at the corner, he insisted that I go with him on over to the church, this I finally did.

When we got to the door I found a nice group of girls, some of whom were ready to scuffle with us for the candy. A few of them, however, took no part in the fun, and among them was my black eyed Hannah Rowley. I offered her some candy which she accepted with thanks, and I sat down beside her and talked, while Leonard was still scuffling with the other girls. It was now time for the meeting and people began to gather. Soon we were crowded over against the wall, and we noticed some people craning their necks to be sure if it was me there with a girl.

So being a good sport, I asked to walk her home, which was two miles above town on the Rowley Flats. She accepted my offer and as we walked along, we talked of our first meeting at the Post Office on the 10th of September 1884. I told her how my wife and I had felt about her at that time, and she said she had the same feeling. And so from that day to this, June 16, 1932, I have never worried about that covenant.

The next day I asked her father, Samuel Rowley, if he had any objections to me getting better acquainted with her. He said if she is satisfied I am and you have my consent.

…We went through the temple on the 25th day of August, 1887 and were married. So the Covenant made by me in 1884 was good, and I have never regretted it—not for once. At the time Hannah was but seventeen years of age, and I had a son Milas only five years younger. I also had four others ranging in age from eleven down to three. She came into my life not only as my wife and companion, but as a mother to the children. She was lovingly called "Aunt Hannah" by her own request. So Aunt Hannah is the title she has been lovingly called every since. And to this day, 1932, they call her blessed.

She has truly been a part of my life. It would be hard to change my mind from the belief that in our first primeval condition we formed a covenant, and were foreordained to come here on earth and have the experience of earth life. Our experiences here have amply proved it.

Alice came into my life so naturally, and was so willing to live the gospel in all its requirements, and even made the choice of her companion in marriage even though a stranger at the time....[7]

Barbara Smith Amussen ~ third wife of Carl Christian Amussen

I was 18 when I married Mr. Amussen. I married him for the Principle; and because he was such a fine character.

His first wife told me afterward how it had been when he talked to her about taking another wife. She said she had not known how to decide, but she finally said to her husband that they ought to make it a subject of prayer. That night they prayed and after she had gone to sleep she had a dream wherein I was married to Mr. Amussen and had brought many children to him. So she gave her consent.

I also had made it a subject of prayer. I had never thought I would marry into polygamy. But I prayed about it and asked for an answer to my prayer and got it. So I was married.[8]

Mary Ann Price Hyde ~ third wife of Orson Hyde

...On the return of Orson Hyde from his mission to Palestine he carried letters of introduction to me and invited me to visit his wife. I was there met by Joseph Smith, the prophet, who, after an interesting conversation introduced the subject of Plural Marriage and endeavored to teach me that principle. I resisted it with every argument I could command, for with my tradition, it was most repulsive to my feelings and rendered me very unhappy as I could not reconcile it with the purity of the gospel of Christ. Mr. Hyde took me home in a carriage and asked me what I thought of it and if I would consent to enter his family? I replied that I could not think of it for a moment.

Thus it rested for a while and Mr. Hyde married another young lady. In the mean time I was trying to learn the character of leading men, for I sincerely hoped they were men of God but, in my mind, plurality of wives was the serious question.

I soon learned to my satisfaction, that Mr. Orson Hyde was a conscientious, upright and noble man and became his third wife. Mrs. Hyde had two sweet little girls and I soon learned to love them and their dear mother who in the spring of 1842 received me into her house as her husband's wife sealed to him by Joseph the prophet in her presence. We lived happily together until our exodus from Nauvoo, when circumstances separated us for a season.

...I will here state that since my first trial in receiving the principle of Plural or Celestial Marriage I have never doubted this being the work of God and <u>know</u> that it is the most "glorious dispensation of the fullness of times" destined to usher in the millennium, when peace shall rein on the earth.

In my forty years experience in this church I have had many testimonies of its divine origin and know for myself that it is the gospel of Jesus Christ. I now occupy the same house where my honored husband breathed his last with two of his wives and their children - four sons and one daughter....[9]

Elizabeth Ann Whitney

My husband revealed these things [*plural marriage*] to me; we had always been united, and had the utmost faith and confidence in each other. We pondered upon them continually, and our prayers were unceasing that the Lord would grant us some special manifestation concerning this new and strange doctrine. The Lord was very merciful to us; He revealed unto us His power and glory. We were seemingly wrapt in a heavenly vision, a halo of light encircled us, and we were convinced in our own minds that God heard and approved our prayers and intercedings before Him.[10]

Benjamin F. Johnson

It was Sunday morning, April 3rd or 4th, 1843, that the Prophet was at my home in Ramus, and after breakfast he proposed a stroll together, and taking his arm, our walk led toward a swail, surrounded by trees and tall brush and near the forest line not far from my house. Through the swail ran a small spring brook, across which a tree was fallen and was clean of its bark. On this we sat down and the Prophet proceeded at once to open to me the subject of plural and eternal marriage and he said that years ago in Kirtland the Lord had revealed to him the ancient order of plural marriage, and the necessity for its practice, and did command that he take another wife, and that among his first thoughts was to come to my mother for some of her daughters. And as he was again required of the Lord to take more wives, he had come now to ask me for my sister Almira.

His words astonished me and almost took my breath. I sat for a time amazed, and finally, almost ready to burst with emotion, I looked him straight in the face and said: "Brother Joseph, this is something I did not expect, and I do not understand it. You know whether it is right, I do not. I want to do just as you tell me, and I will try to, but if I ever should know that you do this to dishonor and debauch my sister, I will kill you as sure as the Lord lives." And while his eyes did not move from mine, he said with a smile, in a soft tone: "But Benjamin you will never know that, but you will know the principle in time, and will finally rejoice in what it will bring to you." "But how," I asked, "can I teach my sister what I myself do not understand, or show her what I do not myself see?" "But you will see and understand it," said he, "And when you open your mouth to talk to your sister, light will come to you and your mouth will be full and your tongue loose, and I will today preach a sermon to you that none but you will understand." Both of these promises were more than fulfilled. The text of his sermon was our use of the "one, five and ten talents," and as God had now commanded plural marriage, and as exaltation and dominion depended upon the number of their righteous posterity, from him who was found but with one talent, it would be taken and given him that had ten, which item of doctrine seems now to be somehow differently construed.

But my thought and wish is to write of things just as they occurred, and I now bear an earnest testimony that his other prediction was more than fulfilled, for when with great hesitation and stammering I called my sister to a private audience, and stood before her shaking with fear, just so soon as I found power to open my mouth, it was filled, for the light of the Lord shone upon my understanding, and the subject that had seemed so dark now appeared of all subjects pertaining to our gospel the most lucid and plain; and so both my sister and myself were converted together, and never again did I need evidence or argument to sustain that high and holy principle. And within a few days of this period my sister accompanied me to Nauvoo, where at my sister Delcena's, we soon met the Prophet with his brother Hyrum and Wm. Clayton as his private secretary, who always accompanied him. Brother

Hyrum at once took me in hand, apparently in fear I was not fully converted, and this was the manner of his talk to me: "Now Benjamin, you must not be afraid of this new doctrine, for it is all right. You know Brother Hyrum don't get carried away by worldly things, and he fought this principle until the Lord showed him it was true. I know that Joseph was commanded to take more wives, and he waited until an angel with a drawn sword stood before him and declared that if he longer delayed fulfilling that command he would slay him." This was the manner of Brother Hyrum's teaching to me, which I then did not need, as I was fully converted....[11]

Son of Joseph C. Bentley

His first wife "Maggie" was a cousin of his second. He and Maggie were married in 1889. She was seven years his junior. At the time he courted his first wife he discussed plural marriage with her, pointing out that he wished her to know that he believed in the "principle" and that he might later feel it his duty to take a plural wife. He said he felt it was only fair to make this matter clear. He was delighted when the young woman replied that she believed in polygamy herself and would not want him as a husband unless he did.

After their marriage in the St. George Temple, he lived there or nearby for a year. His wife suggested he take her cousin Gladys Woodsmansee as a second wife. Gladys was older than Maggie, being only two years Bentley's junior. The suggestion was well received by the husband and he followed up on the same very shortly. Gladys later (after the marriage as I understood it), told Bentley that she had hoped and planned for a literary career, that she wanted to write stories, etc., and that she had no desire to be married. However, one night she had a dream in which she saw a cluster of five lovely children in the air above her head. This dream convinced her that she should marry and bear children.[12]

Charles Ramsden Bailey

Following a short marriage and divorce to a girl who left him for another, Charles R. Bailey related the following story.

Bro. Standiford and I were sleeping in the wagon and I dreamed that I was about to marry again and I was going to marry two wives. One I had seen and was able to place her but the other I had not as yet seen or met. When I awakened I told Brother Standiford about my dream. He said it was strange. I went to sleep and dreamed the same thing over again. Then I dreamed it the third time. I was not very much in favor of polygamy for I had lived with families in plural marriage and could see it was really something for men and women to live it. But I went along, thinking about my dream and the promise made by Peter Maughan and sometimes wondered if there could be anything to it. I thought I would leave it in the hands of God.

In the latter part of June we arrived at Florence and found a large crowd of people there. After we had been there for two weeks, six of us were standing at a store and three young ladies came along. I remarked: "Boys, here comes the girl who will be my wife." The boys looked at me and said: "Which one ?" I answered: "The middle one." The boys said: "You have never spoken to her yet." I answered, "No, but I will." They all laughed at me. However, in a few days we went to a dance and I spoke to her, but she found it hard to make me understand.

She would say: "Nix Fursts" and I began to wonder about my dreams of two years ago and if there was anything to it. In a few days Thomas Leishman told me that my girl was gone in the Sanpete Company. "Now," said he, "what about what you said at the store that time?" I told him I did not know why I said it, and if it were not to be her, it would have to be someone else.

One morning I awoke and said to Joseph Kay, my bed mate: "Let's go to town today. What for I do not know but I feel I must go." After breakfast we went after some of the cattle, and had quite a time to get them, but we finally succeeded and then went down to Florence—five miles away. As soon as we got to the store Brother Cluff, who had charge of the Scandinavian Saints asked us if we were from the Cache Valley company. We told him "Yes." He asked us if we could take some folks that were camped out there as they wanted to go in our company. We said, "Yes," and told Joseph Kay to go after them. I said to Joseph: "I'll bet you my girl is with them." So he started after them and in a short time I saw him coming back with them. He waved his whip and hat and I knew she was with him. They rode in Joseph Kay's wagon all the way and we were close by all the time.

Early in July we started back for Utah. We did not have many emigrants in our company. We had about 15 kegs of nails for the Salt Lake Tabernacle. We made good time until we arrived at Sweetwater. Feed was very scare as it had been a dry summer. The cattle began to get thin; many of them took sick and died. A teamster really feels bad to see this happen. After a hard journey we arrived in Salt Lake and got unloaded. Now I did not know whether Johannah and her mother, Mrs. Adamson, were going to stop in Salt Lake or go to Cache with me. I let them think about it. They had had such a good time while we were unloading and made many friends. When I was ready to leave I asked them whether they wanted to stay here or go with me and they said they wanted to go with me.

We started and in three days, Sept. 27, we were in Wellsville. Then trouble commenced, if I dare call it such. I had a girl at home that I had been keeping company with for a year and a half. However, I tried to keep cool and tried to keep things level. After everyone had said what they wanted, I started in and said what I wanted to say. I remember the first night I took Susannah Hawkins home from singing practice. The gate was standing open and Mother Hawkins told me to leave at once. Making so much noise I thought I had better obey. In the morning Brother Samuel Obery, who lived very close to Mother Hawkins, went over and asked her what she was making such a noise about the night before. She told him. "Well, you did wrong," he told her. "Why so," she said and he answered, "I was thinking about the matter and a voice said, 'Charles is going to marry both those girls,' and so you must encourage it." She said no more, but was willing to give her to me and I now saw my dream coming to pass.

About the 20th of October I went to President Peter Maughan and took the girls (Johannah Adamson and Susannah Hawkins), with me and asked him for a recommend to go to the Endowment House and take these two for wives. "Yes," he said cheerfully. Then he remarked: "Did I not promise this to you?" [*Three and a half years earlier President Maugham had promised Charles upon his divorce, "Be faith-*

ful and I will promise that you will marry again. You will marry two faithful Latter-day Saint girls and will raise a large family."] He said: "I felt it in my very bones and thank God it came to pass. Go on, you have my blessings." In spite of all the opposition and peculiar circumstances from the time I had my dream, it was fulfilled on the 17th day of November, 1863.

I may add it was the grandest step of my life, and while it brought its many cares and trials, I never felt it as such. Many things might have been avoided had we known better, but we had to learn by experience. By proving faithful and true to the end, the promise is sure, no matter who may say to the contrary. I have narrated my courtship and marriage to show to my family that I was not the instigator of this matter for I was not fully converted to the principle of polygamy but I was brought to see it in a marvelous way, to believe it and obey it.[13]

Elizabeth Mears Hawkins Mortensen ~ second wife of James Mortensen

Elizabeth Mears Hawkins Mortensen, daughter Thomas Hawkins and Elizabeth Mears, was born March 1, 1867 at Salt Lake City, Utah. She was the second child of family of five children. Her people first lived in Salt Lake City after arriving from England in the year 1853. Here they lived until 1869, when they moved on south to Lehi, Utah, helping in the colonization of that place. Then after ten years in Lehi, they moved further south into Arizona, helping settle Taylor, Arizona.

By this time Elizabeth was a real Pioneer, and at the age of fourteen was helping to support the family by working for different people. She became well acquainted with everybody in Taylor and Snowflake, and evidently attended school in Taylor. Her school days were limited, due to pioneer living, and having to help support the family.

She chanced to help or work now and then for Ida Jane Pease Mortensen, in the home of James Mortensen, and thus became well acquainted with this lovely family, and they learned to love and appreciate her very much, as she was pleasant and earnest in her work.

At the age of seventeen past, she had become a lovely young lady, and because of the practice of plurality of wives among her people, members of the Church of Jesus Christ of Latter Day Saints, it fell to her lot to become the second wife of a wonderful God fearing man, James Mortensen.

The story goes, that she worked for the Mortensen family off and on, they realized what a wonderful person she was; so Ida Jane picked her as a suitable second wife for her husband James. Then James started courting her with the approval of his first wife. He was practical in all that he undertook to do. She rode with him in the wagon, as he broke or trained his horses. An old timer of that area who knew the James Mortensen family well told me of this. After a period of courting or courtship, the whole Mortensen and Hawkins tribes planned and took the long trip by wagon and team to St. George, Utah, where they witnessed the wedding and sealing of James and Elizabeth for Time and all Eternity in the "House of the Lord" on the 22nd day of December 1884.

Plurality was the order of the day and if they were worthy, members were asked to live it, James, Ida and Elizabeth covenanted with each other to live, love and respect one another, and they did. Each wife had nine children and her own home. James was a very just and honest man; there was no partiality shown either wife, they really loved and respected one another as if they were really blood sisters.[14]

George Darling Watt
Letter of proposal to Elizabeth Golightly from George Darling Watt.

Elizabeth,

The subject upon which I now venture to address you is one pregnant with serious interest to a young woman whose maturity would point out a duty enjoined upon her by the revealed laws of God and of Nature: mainly, the choice of a companion with whom she can spend her life, and with whom, if necessary, suffer all things for the love she bares him.

I offer myself to you, if you can in return give me this love, and with it yourself, which offering would be prized by me above the glittering and perishable treasures of earth.

I have visited you oft of late; you have seen me as I am, and you may have formed an opinion of me detrimental to the fulfillment of my wishes; I have not tried to deceive you by false appearances. I have my weaknesses, but if the love and purity of the soul remains unimpaired, the weaknesses of the flesh are always pardonable. With such a love I

Photo used by permission, Utah State Historical Society, all rights reserved.

can love you. If you can give me in return such an affection, it will cover a multitude of faults, and make us happy in each other.

Perhaps I ought to say, that Alice respects you, and loves you next to her own Sisters, and more than any young woman she is acquainted with. As to her disposition, and natural goodness of heart I need not say a word, for you are acquainted with her enough to know what she is for yourself. With the other question of my family you are not so well acquainted.

I would like to know your mind upon this matter, that if my visits as a suitor may not be allowed I may cease forthwith to trouble you, and to deceive myself with expectations that can never be realized, but as before continue my few and far between visits as an old friend and Bro.

God bless you is the earnest prayer
of your ever affectionate Bro. in the Gospel.
Geo. D. Watt

P.S. I have mentioned the matter to your father who gave me leave to pay my addresses to you in as much as you wished it.[15]

Isaiah M. Coombs

...It was in January 1860 that my wife and I began to talk seriously about obeying the Celestial law in relation to plural marriage. She was not only willing, but anxious for me to take other wives, notwithstanding our poverty, as she understood perfectly that unless we rendered obedience to that order of things that we would forfeit all right to claim each other as husband and wife after the resurrection. With this understanding, I made at least two efforts, while living in Parowan, to obtain wives. The time, however, had not arrived for me to enter into that holy order and I failed in my efforts. I record this fact here that our children may know how early in life their noble and self-sacrificing mother accepted, as an article of her faith this order of plural marriage so despised by the world, but so necessary to the exaltation of man and woman. So I have today taken to myself as wife for time and all eternity, Charlotte Augusta Hardy. Augusta was born April 7, 1851 in Mansfield, Nottingham, England. Her mother is long since dead. Her maiden name was Charlotte Augusta Birchby. Her father's name is John Thomas Hardy.

July 1st (1875). On this day I brought into our home my wife, Charlotte Augusta Hardy. This was with the full and free consent of my first wife, Fanny, who gave her a cordial greeting to the home she had helped to make and furnish. Next day after Augusta's arrival, Fanny took her through the house and showing her all that we had been able by long-time economy and labor to accumulate to make our home comfortable, told her, "All this belongs to the family. You are now one of us, so take hold and use and enjoy all that you see the same as the rest of us. Everything there is here, except what is in my private bedroom, belongs as much to you as to me. I want to see you feel at home." This speech came from the heart of my peerless wife. She meant every word of it and her actions ever afterwards proved her sincerity. Augusta was treated by Fanny and her children as an honored guest. Fanny led out in this and taught her children how they should demean themselves toward their father's wife.[16]

Jane T. Bleak ~ third wife of James G. Bleak

When I came to Utah it was with an independent company. I wanted to come and father had written to Brother Bleak saying I wanted to come. Brother Bleak said for me to come and stay with him and his wife until Father was ready to join us. So I came ahead. It was with an independent company and we had a very pleasant time crossing the plains. I don't remember any hardships. Each day we traveled as far as we could and we had plenty to eat. At night we would put the wagons together—you've seen pictures of the way they did—and we would sing and dance and have meetings and prayer. There were good musicians there. We had good times. My brother came with me and when we got in Salt Lake (August, 1861), Brother Bleak came to  meet us. He said, "Where's Jenny?" they called me that when I was a child, and my brother said, "This is Jenny." He couldn't believe it. He thought I'd be a child like I was when he left England. I was just fifteen though I looked sixteen, I was so strong and well developed.

I lived with them and they were called to go to Dixie. Brother Bleak had two wives then and Brigham Young called him in and said,

"James," he called him James, "You are going down to Dixie and heaven only knows when you will get back here. You ought to take a third wife so you will have a family circle." In those days men were advised to take three wives to make a circle. They thought it was best. Brother Bleak said, "Brother Brigham, I don't want to get married and I don't feel that I should. It's only been a year since I married Carolyn and I don't feel that I can possibly support anther family. And don't know what it will be like in the new country." "That's why you need another wife," Brigham Young said, "You will need your family there. And it's a commandment that has been put upon us and which we must obey. I know it will be hard but you marry and the way will be opened before you."

I think that the country needed populating. They had to have big families and that was the only way to have them. And it was a commandment from God and had to be obeyed. People can't understand it now. Then we gave up everything we had and obeyed the leaders implicitly. When Brigam said a thing we did it, just like he was an angel from heaven. After we had given up everything for our faith it wasn't hard to accept another commandment. We did it without question. Nowadays women don't have that kind of faith. I don't like to talk about polygamy because the younger people ridicule it. Everything was so different then and they can't understand it. People are not like they were and they can't understand why we did the things we did, but it was because we had our faith.

Brigham asked Brother Bleak if there wasn't a young woman he would like to marry and he said "No, he didn't want to marry." Then Brigham asked him if there wasn't a young woman among the immigrants he would like. Brother Bleak said "No" and then he thought of me and told Brigham that I was pretty young to be married, but that maybe I would. He said, too, he didn't like to marry me until he had talked with my father. But Brigham said that was too long to wait and for him to go marry me and it would be all right. He asked me and I said, "No, I don't want to marry you or anybody else. I'm too young to marry and besides I would not marry without my father and mother being here." He didn't press me any farther and he told Brigham what I said. Brother Brigham said, "James, you bring the young lady here in the morning and I'll talk to her." Of course, I went. I wouldn't have thought of anything else.

When we got there Brigham had a mischievous twinkle in his eye and he said, "So! You don't want to marry James?" I said, "No, I don't want to marry anybody." Then he asked me if there was anybody else I cared for and I told him that I didn't know anybody else. Then he talked to me and told me about it being a commandment and how we would be blessed if we followed it and lived up to it and if we didn't we would be condemned. He said that if I did it I would be blessed and happy and never regret it. He said it would be all right with my parents and that it was the thing to do. He convinced me and we were married in October and went to St. George in November....Brother Bleak was good and just to his wives.[17]

Samuel Amos Woolley

...During the winter I went to school to Professor O. Pratt for near two months, worked in the stone quarry getting out stone for to build the Temple with for over one month. J. M. [*John Mills Woolley*] and I worked together and went to school together too. We dug a cellar on a lot E. D. [*Edwin Dilworth Woolley*] bot and built upon, worked some on the island cutting wood, etc. Thus I spent the winter. Early the next spring which was 1842, E. D. had the house built on the lot he had bot of Joseph. He then enlarged his merchandise business, so that I was employed therein....

I spent the summer of 1843 in the above named business. I generally had a spell of sickness each summer or fall. This fall I had a very severe spell, so that I lay for some time not expected to live, but with the blessing of the Lord my life was spared. Brothers Joseph, Hyrum and some of the authorities visited me almost daily, and administered to me, etc. The disease was then intermitary fever mostly in the head.

The most of the folks that saw me thot I could never get well again. During the time of my sickness, Bro. Joseph and Hyrum commenced to teach Edwin and his family the principle of the plurality of wives. They say I was taken sick I heard E. D. and Bro. Hyrum talking about something that I could not understand at all as I only heard a word now and then and was very sick. That day I lay downstairs on the bed, E. D. and his wife slept in, so when it came night, I went upstairs and did not come down again for some weeks. After I commenced to get a little better, or at least the fever had left me, but still I could not raise myself in bed, there was quite a singular circumstance took place which can only be ascribed to the power of God.

I do not know the day of the month but it was in October in 1843. Edwin and his wife being desirous of seeing and hearing read the revelation which had been given to Joseph, commanding him and others to take a plurality of wives (the revelation was given on the 12th of May), which thing was altogether contrary to our traditions, the promise was made to them that they should see and hear it, so Hyrum came and read it to them. Before doing so (as it was a private thing at that time), all the doors were shut and fastened. The store door and shutters were fastened too as it joined the house. The blinds of the room windows were dropped so that it would have the appearance of no one being at home. The stair door which usually was kept open and generally someone was with me, was now closed (and no one left in my room), for fear I could hear it, and being sick it might worry me at first. Still I was so bad I did not know my friends when they came to see me, but after all this precaution being taken I saw and heard as much as any one of them, and when I got well I could tell (and did), all about it. How each one acted and where each one sat (which they acknowledged was true). I told them and showed them the very spot where Bro. Hyrum sat and read the revelation and where I stood behind him....

But I am like St. Paul of old, whether in the body or out of the body I cannot tell, but one thing I do know, and others can bear witness that I both saw and heard, from what I told them afterwards. This is the testimony I have had with regard to a plurality of wives being from God.[18]

After the marriage to Catharine E. Mehring in May of 1846, Samuel embraced the principle and married Francis Ann Phillips and Elizabeth Ann Stephenson.

Margaret McNeil Ballard ~ first wife of Henry Ballard

On the 27th of April, 1856, we left Liverpool, England for America.…We were on the ocean six weeks and landed at Castle Garden, New York. Because of mother's condition and my being the eldest member of the family, and being blessed with good health, I had to share the responsibility with my father of taking care of the children.…After landing, we planned to go west with a handcart company, but President Franklin D. Richards counseled father not to go with that company, for which we were afterwards thankful. My father was then advised to go to St. Louis and spend the winter there and prepare to go to Utah the next year.

We had not gone far when we met Patriarch John Smith and Brother John P. Green…Brother Smith told father to leave the company and go on as fast as it was possible for it was getting cold and we were short of food. He also said to go through Weber Canyon to Ogden and stay there until he had earned enough food to put us through the winter. Then go to Cache Valley and take up land. We started out on our journey alone and had a very hard time of it. Our food gave out and we had nothing but milk and wild rose berries to eat. However, we had a good team and could travel fast.

We arrived in Ogden on the 4th day of October. We camped on the outskirts of the town while father went on into Ogden to find work… Across the field from where we were was a little house and out in the yard was a big pile of squash. We were all nearly starved to death. My mother sent me over to this place to beg a squash, for we did not have a cent of money and some of the children were very weak for the want of food. I knocked at the door and an old lady came and said, "Come in, come in, I knew you were coming and have been told to give you food." She gave me a large loaf of fresh bread and said to tell my mother that she would come over soon. It was not long until she came and brought us a nice cooked dinner, something we had not had for a long time. The woman was surely inspired of the Lord to help us and we were indeed grateful for her kindness. When father came back to us, he had found a man whom he had known in Scotland. This man took us to his home and we stayed there until we were ready to go to Cache Valley.

When we had sufficient supplies we left Ogden and had not gone far when we met Henry Ballard and Aaron DeWitt who had been to conference and were returning to their homes in Cache Valley. This was my first meeting with my future husband.

At the time of this meeting I was a barefooted, sunburned little girl, driving my cow along the road, but it was made known to mother and my future husband at that time that I would someday be his wife. They helped us greatly on our journey and we traveled together to Cache Valley. We arrived in Logan on October 21st, 1859. We camped in a fort for protection against the Indians.

In January, Brother Ballard asked me to go to a dance with him over at Providence, a little village three miles from Logan. We had a yoke of oxen and a heavy sleigh and it was very cold. It snowed while we were in the canyon to the depth of three feet. We could not go home so we sat up all the rest of the night, for there was not room for so many of us to go to bed in one little log house. We had a very hard time to get home the next day, so you see even courting in pioneer days had its hardships.

I had been keeping company with Brother Ballard for sometime, and although I was but fifteen years old, he wanted me to marry him. He felt that he could take care of me and provide for me without having to work so hard. We were married on May 5, 1861. He was put in as Bishop of the Logan Second Ward on April 14th of that year, which position he held for nearly forty years, during which time I tried to assist and encourage him in his work.

The law of plural marriage had now been made manifest by revelation to the servants of God. My husband, being a Bishop, had been counseled by the authorities to set the example of obedience by entering into this law. The compliance of this was a greater trial to my husband than it was to me. He would say, "Margaret, you are the only woman in the world I ever want."…While this was a trial for both of us we knew that the Lord expected us to be obedient in this law, as in all laws, as revealed in these, the latter days.

After many weeks of pondering and praying for guidance, I persuaded my husband to enter into this law and suggested to him my sister, Emily, three years younger than myself, as his second wife. This was agreeable to him for she was a beautiful, lovable girl of eighteen years. During their courtship he was manly, honorable, and upright toward both me and my sister. Never once did he neglect me or leave me alone during this time. Many times he took me to my mother's with my babies to spend the evening while he took Emily to a dance, and at all times showed me every courtesy and consideration.

They decided to be married in October in the Endowment House. Henry asked me to go with them on this trip. I made a protest as I was in a delicate condition. Henry was grieved and said to me, "Margaret, unless you go with me and give your consent to this marriage and stand as a witness, I will not go." I went and made the trip in a covered wagon over a hundred miles of rough road and gave my consent and blessing to the union. Thus, on October 4, 1867, my husband married my sister, Emily, for his second wife, sealed for time and eternity. Although I loved my sister dearly, and we knew it was a commandment of God that we should live in celestial marriage, it was a great trial and sacrifice to me. But the Lord blessed and comforted me and we lived happily in this principle of the Gospel. On May 15th, 1868, I gave birth to twin babies, a boy and girl.[19]

David King Udall

In the autumn of 1881, while I was acting as superintendent of the Co-op Store in St. Johns, I was instrumental in employing as bookkeeper and clerk, Miss Ida Hunt, daughter of Bishop John Hunt of Snowflake. My acquaintance with her proved her to be a womanly woman with an abiding faith in the Gospel. She was a charming girl with a wealth of auburn hair and the gift of song.

Before the winter had passed and with Ella's knowledge and consent I talked with Ida about becoming my plural wife. In doing this I conformed to a deep conviction of the divinity of the doctrine of plural marriage—a conviction I had reached in studying the Gospel while I was on my mission. In accepting Joseph Smith as a prophet of God, logically I accepted the revelation given to him in the Doctrine and Covenants, Section 132 on the new and everlasting covenant of marriage, which included the plurality of wives.

Ella and I had both been reared in homes where there was more than one wife and one mother. Ella told me during our courtship that she believed the doctrine of plural marriage to be uplifting and divine. This belief was a natural reaction to her happy home life in her father's large family. The test now came to Ella and it proved to be a severe trial to her. How could it have been otherwise for she was to divide my love with another woman. She was sustained in meeting this experience with a firm faith in the righteousness of the principle.

I was sorely tried myself. It hurt me in an inexplainable way to cause Ella any heartache… Only the deepest religious conviction on the part of all of us could have sustained us in consummating the plan. In the spring Ida gave up her work in the A.C.M.I. and returned to her home in Snowflake where she resumed her work of school teaching for a month or two.

Speaking of trials, I was once tempted in view of the many obstacles in our way to give up the whole plan. I had written Ida I expected to call by Snowflake on my way home from a business trip to Holbrook; she was to give me her final word and I was to ask her parents' approval. Very distinctly I recall my feelings as I approached the forks of the road east of Woodruff. One road led to Snowflake where Ida was awaiting me; the other road led to St. Johns—to my home, my wife and baby. For a little time my mind was undecided and my soul in torment. I dismounted and on my knees prayed fervently that I might be guided aright. A calm assurance came over me and I knew it was my duty and privilege to enter into plural marriage. I whipped up my horse and rode to Snowflake as fast as the darkness would permit. From that day to this I have felt that in accepting plural marriage we have fulfilled the plan of Heaven for me and mine. It was the will of God to us.

On May 6, 1882, I started on a second wedding trip. It was in another covered wagon, but this time it was to increase not to begin my family circle. Ella showed her good sportsmanship by complying with my urgent request that she go with us to the St. George Temple in southern Utah where Ida and I were to be married. It was an unusual trip. The girls read several books aloud as we jogged slowly over the desert. Baby Pearl was talking and proved to be our safety valve in conversation. At night in my roll of camp bedding I slept on the ground guarding the wagon in which my precious ones were sleeping. In contemplating the future, as I lay there under the stars, I realized I was placing myself in the crucible to be tested for better or for worse. With all my faith I prayed constantly that I might measure up to the standard that Ella and Ida had a right to expect of me. My heart went out in great tenderness to my two brave sweet girls.

Wives of David King Udall

The following letters are correspondence between David King Udall's prospective bride Ida, and his first wife Ella.

Dear Sister:

I feel that I cannot allow another day to pass by without writing you to ascertain if possible your true feelings upon a subject which is, no doubt, one painful to us both, but one which, I realize, must be disposed of sooner or later, viz: the possibility or probability of my becoming at some future day a member of your family. I trust you will not consider it presuming in me addressing you without permission. In doing so I have consulted only my own sense of duty and right, feeling that I cannot allow the matter to go farther, without first having received some assurance of your willingness to such a step being taken, at least that you have no more serious objections to me than you would to any other under like circumstances.

During my stay in St. Johns I learned to love you as a sister, and the very thought that I may have been the cause of bringing unhappiness to you has troubled me day and night. Nothing but pride kept me from writing this letter long ago. But I have finally become convinced that such humiliation is nothing compared to that of receiving the attentions of any man contrary to the wishes of his wife.

I trust, dear sister, that you will appreciate my true motive in writing and favor me with an answer if only a few words. I believe in this matter, it is not only your right, but your imperative duty to state plainly any objections you may have in your feelings and I beg you will not hesitate to do so. I promise you I shall not be offended, but on the contrary, shall thank you for it all my life, and I believe you will not have written in vain, for, unless it meets with your approval, I shall never listen to another word on the subject.

May the Lord bless you and help you to decide in this matter is the earnest prayer of—

Your true friend,
Ida Hunt

Ella's response:

Dear Friend:

I received your letter bearing date of January 29th some weeks ago. My health has been so very poor that I have felt unable to reply sooner and am scarcely equal to the task now.

The subject in question has caused me a great amount of pain and sorrow, more perhaps than you could imagine, yet I feel as I have from the beginning, that if it is the Lord's will I am perfectly willing to try to endure it and trust it will be overruled for the best good of all. My feelings are such that I can write but briefly on this subject.

With kind regards to all, I remain your friend,
E. L. Udall

Ida Hunt Udall ~ second wife of David King Udall
An excerpt from Ida's journal regarding her plural marriage.

...On the evening of Saturday, May 6, 1882, I left my dearly beloved home in Snowflake, Arizona, in company with Brother and Sister D. K. Udall, and their baby Pearl, to make a short visit to Utah.... We put up with Sister Udall's brother, Tommy Stewart, whose second wife is a sister of Brother Udall. Unfortunately he was not at home, but his two pretty, young wives gave us a hearty welcome.

Spent a pleasant evening in conversation, songs and music. But with all the merriment, I felt lonely and depressed like a stranger in a strange land. The sorrow another was passing through, seemingly on my account (though I was powerless to help it), the constant strain my mind had been on during the whole journey lest by word or look I should cause her unnecessary unhappiness, had weighed upon my spirits greatly and I retired from the scene that evening with a feeling of dread and fear at my heart impossible to describe. Afterward I was greatly reassured by a moonlight walk and conversation with the one dearest on earth to me, who brought light and hope to my heart once more, with his loving, encouraging words. I finally went to bed, feeling that in striving to obey the commandments of God with a pure motive.

I had everything to live for. No matter how severe the trial, what a privilege to pass through it, in such a glorious cause....May 25. This afternoon at half-past five o'clock, in the Holy Temple of the Lord, I was sealed for Time and all Eternity to David King Udall, the only man on earth to whose care I could freely and gladly entrust my future, for better or worse....

Marriage, under ordinary circumstances is a grave and important step, but entering into Plural Marriage, in these perilous times is doubly so. May Heaven help me to keep the vows I have made sacred and pure, and may the deep unchangeable love which I feel for my husband today increase with every coming year, helping me to prove worthy of the love and confidence which he imposes in me, and to always be just and considerate to those the Lord has given unto him. When he bade me goodnight the sacred name of "wife" was whispered for the first time in my ear, causing my heart to flutter with a strange and new happiness.[20]

Belinda Marden Pratt ~ sixth wife of Parley P. Pratt

In my mind I had accepted all the revelations of God, plural marriage included, but on account of the sayings and doings of some of the brothers and sisters, I suffered the temptations of Satan to nearly overcome me so far that I thought I would have nothing to do with it. I mean Celestial Marriage. A good sister where I was staying called in President Young to talk to me. He instructed me in the principle and desiring with all my heart to understand the truth, I testify that the Holy Spirit of God rested down upon me and it was made plain to my understanding that it was a divine principle and with great joy of heart I accepted it and never from that time to this, 1889, has there been doubt in my mind concerning it. I married Parley P. Pratt on or about the 20th of November 1844, at the house of Erastus Snow....[21]

William Hyde
A plural marriage proposal to Abigail Gloyd and Sarah Pratt.

Lehi City, Nov. 12, 1859

Sisters,

It may be somewhat to your surprise that I address you at so early a period of an acquaintance, on the subject of so much importance as the one that calls for these few lines, but I trust that in your kindness you will pardon my presumption if a presumption it may be called. When I first heard that a couple of ladies that I baptized had come into the city, the thought came into my mind that I would like to see you and

I had made arrangements to go to the city for that purpose, but circumstances have been so arranged to bring you to my humble home where could it please my Heavenly Father to implant within you a desire to remain through time, and throughout all Eternity, I should truly be grateful. This is coming to the subject in rather a blunt way is it not, but why not as well that way as any other.

It is true that I have not an over abundance of this world to offer you, but should both of you or either of you be pleased or rather conclude to comply with my suggestion, I will promise that through the mercy of God, it shall not only be that with me you have commenced in the first ordinances of the Gospel but with me you shall be saved and exalted in the Kingdom of our Father and I will say further, (which I feel to do the more cheerfully from the knowledge I have of my past labors and desires to do right). But on my part no reasonable pains shall be spared to procure to you comfort and happiness in time, but the result of all my labors, including that of writing these lines, I must leave in the hands of God. Praying, however, that in his goodness he will reward me in mercy, your love, and integrity for the truth have their affect to endear you to me and we may, if we chose so to do, learn to love each other more perfectly.

Please consider the above prayerfully and don't be angry with me for this writing and allow me—

Respectfully to subscribe myself
Your friend and brother in the Gospel
William Hyde

Second proposal letter to Sarah Pratt.

December 19, 1859
Lehi, Utah

Sister Sarah,

I have concluded to trouble you a little with some of my thoughts upon paper, but with a sincere desire that the little trouble to which I do put you may not be so very painful. Since I last saw you I have had many reflections, and in reference to your real feelings I hardly know what conclusions to form, but let them be as they may there is one thing which I consider justifiable in me to state, and that is, that it is my wish that you should act in all things in accordance with that light which accompanies the Gospel which we have embraced, which light it is your privilege to have, and not that you should feel that you are rather compelled by the force of circumstances to move in a direction which is not in accordance with the light which is within you. This, Sarah, you have no occasion to do, for the Heavens will bare me witness that it is not my feeling that you will ever be left without friends and home in the valleys of the mountains.

It is true that we have embraced the Gospel of this the Holy Ghost, as well as all things which we behold bares record. It is also true that if we will obtain a full and complete salvation we must abide the law through which that salvation is obtained for thus it is written. Could we always see things in the light of Heaven we should have no trouble in embracing them, but it is necessary that in all things there should be an opposition, otherwise there would be no trial of our faith, and without a trial of our faith and without an experience we could not be perfected.

In reference to the proposition which I have made you it is my feeling that it would be right and acceptable in the sight of God, and if I am not much mistaken when you have the most of the Spirit of the Lord your feelings are inclined in the same channel. But of the powers that oppose us just think of the Devil's showing our Savior all the kingdoms of this world, and then let me ask how much life he shows us when our reflections are in the opposite channel to the Gospel—but Sarah, let nothing move you; let not the powers that oppose us present before you the imperfections of men, and thereby discourage you, but keep the light within you, and be sure that you have that to guide you, and with all be decided for the truth. And should it be your mind to unite your interest with mine, both for time and for all Eternity, it shall be my constant prayer and study to do all in my power for your happiness and salvation as well as for all whom the Lord has or may give me. But truly I feel that my strength is in the Lord, but a knowledge of his word on the subject above referred is that it shall be followed with blessings, and the knowledge that He has blessed me gives me unshaken confidence that I shall be blessed and prospered in as much as I do right.

Well, lest I weary you I guess I may as well stop writing but did I know what to say for your comfort I would gladly write more. May the God of all the faithful be the God of Sarah and Abigail, and may his blessings be upon you forever, and in nothing may you come short of the richness of those blessings and that salvation which the Heavens have in store for the faithful.

                    Faithfully,
                    Your brother in the Gospel,
                    William Hyde[22]

Marriner Wood Merrill

When I was a boy of nine years my mother sent me to the hayfield where my father and brothers were at work, to call them to dinner. On the way I became unconscious and was clothed with a vision which I distinctly remembered when I gained my usual feelings and thoughts. After I became conscious I found myself in a log cabin located on the way to the field. In this cabin I was on my knees in the attitude of prayer. In the vision I saw the Church and the Prophets Joseph and Brigham. I saw the travels of the latter and of the Saints from Nauvoo and Winter Quarters to Utah. In the vision the sight of covered buggies and wagons was peculiar to me, for at that time I had never seen such vehicles, nor had I ever seen the mules which I beheld in my vision. I saw two and sometimes six mules to a wagon, and in the company of pioneers I beheld two men who had been boy friends of my youth, and each of them had more than one wife. In my vision at that time the divinity of plural marriage was revealed to me. I comprehended the doctrines and principles as they had been revealed.

The progress and development of the Church were shown and the persecutions of the Saints were made clear to my understanding, and I heard a voice which told me that all I beheld was true, but I was cautioned to keep to myself what I had seen until I should have the opportunity of leaving my native country. Upon reaching home I was pale, and it was some time

Photo used by permission, Utah State Historical Society, all rights reserved.

before I could speak distinctly. That incident of my life made a very strong impression upon my boyish mind, and one day I ventured to ask my mother a question about plural marriage, why it was not practiced now as in the days of God's ancient people. She answered in surprise by asking what I knew about such things. Fearing that I might betray that secret revealed, I made no more mention of the matter.[23]

Caroline Mariah Carpenter ~ plural wife of Orson Smith

...I always felt I was cut out for polygamy. My father was in polygamy, and I had my own ideas about it. I had plenty of chances to get married before Mr. Smith asked me, but I never found a family where I loved the woman as well as I loved the man. Sometimes I loved the woman more than I loved the man. But to make polygamy successful, you've got to love the man and the woman both as well. That is why I married Mr. Smith.[24]

George Teasdale

And as far as I am concerned as an individual, not one principle that God has revealed from the heavens do I dare to go back on—not one principle. I believe in the fullness of the everlasting Gospel. I believe in plural marriage as a part of the Gospel, just as much as I believe in baptism by immersion for the remission of sins. The same Being who taught me baptism for the remission of sins, taught me plural marriage, and its necessity and glory.

I bear my solemn testimony that plural marriage is as true as any principle that has bean revealed from the heavens. I bear my testimony that it is a necessity, and that the Church of Christ in its fullness never existed without it. Where you have the eternity of marriage you are bound to have plural marriage; bound to; and it is one of the marks of the Church of Jesus Christ in its sealing ordinances. "Whatever you bind on earth is bound in heaven."[25]

Helen Mar Whitney

If I did not know that my husband was actuated by the purest of motives and by religious principle I could not have fortified myself against that "demon Jealousy," and had it not been for a powerful testimony from the Lord, which gave me a knowledge for myself that this principle is of celestial birth, I do not believe that I could have submitted to it for a moment. Therefore I can take no credit to myself, only as far as I rendered obedience to Him. I was afraid of no man, but I feared to rebel against the Almighty, though at times it was like the tearing of my very heart-strings, and it took much prayer and struggling to overcome. Yet through it all I have stood as a pillar by the side of my husband and can say with truth that my soul has been purified and my love has become more exalted. My willing and undivided heart is laid upon the altar, and all my life and talents which the Lord has lent me, I wish to be devoted to this great and glorious cause.[26]

76 ⌒⌒ *More Than One...*

Wives of Joseph Summerhays

Chapter Four

THE JOYS AND BLESSINGS

...being proud of my husband and loving him very much, knowing him to be a man of God and believing he would not love them less because he loved me more.[1]

~ *Bathsheba Smith*

As the Church began to grow, the principle of plural marriage became established and accepted as a basic tenet of the gospel. Many couples who had been brought together by divine direction for the very purpose of uniting in plural marriage, saw their dreams realized and their promises fulfilled. Each would gain a testimony of this sacred principle—the joys and blessings, as well as the sacrifices and sorrows, that would gain for them exaltation in the Lord's kingdom. As a consequence of these experiences came the following affirmations of family life from both husbands and wives. In the end, personal growth, sisterhood, and eternal love would find no equal. The challenges of today would bring the blessings of tomorrow—blessings of *more than one*.

Julia Sarah Abegg Call ~ fourth wife of Anson B. Call

I don't know even yet just what the Lord intended by polygamy, why he asked us to live in it, but I am glad I did. I married in it because it was a privilege.…Polygamy has made me always think of something other than myself. I have had to share my husband's love and in a way my children, but it has given me many things in return. I don't know how to say it but when Velen or one of the other children embrace me, I have the sense of the richness it has brought me. I have the love of all of Aunt Theressa's children, and they come to me with their troubles and their joys and it increases my life. And I know that my children go to Aunt Theressa too. I've been able to say a word to help her children, and to talk to them about some of the things they were doing, so that it would save her worry and sorrow, and she has done the same for me. Aunt Theressa has always been a joy and a comfort to me. She said…that if we had only a crust of bread, we would share it together.[2]

Daughters of John Brown

It is hard today for people to understand polygamy, so we seldom mention it. But in those days people believed it was a divine principle. Father and Auntie were in love with each other, they did not need any one else, and they satisfied each other. But they chose polygamy. I do not know for certain, but I have always understood that Brigham Young asked or advised people to marry in it. There was always a small portion of people in polygamy but almost all of the men who held positions in the Church were polygamists. Father didn't marry again because he was in love with the girl, but because he thought it was his duty and of course it was also possible for him to love his other wives. I know it was hard for Auntie, but she gave her consent and made up

her mind she would live in it. They made up their minds they would live in it for the rest of their lives and they prepared for it.

Both Aunt Amy and Mother were mature enough to know what they were doing. They were attractive girls and had plenty of beaus. In fact they were both engaged to young men. They decided that they wanted to live in polygamy and they admired Father. He was a bright man and a kind man and they wanted him enough to marry him in polygamy. Father was a wise man and he chose wisely. All three of his wives had the same ideas.

…they were all thoughtful of each other. They knew that they had to consider the other's rights. There is nothing in the world so good as polygamy to make people unselfish, once they make up their minds that they will live in it for the rest of their lives.…Whenever one of the wives were ill, another wife would take care of her. It made them all bigger women than they would have been and keeping three women loving him and happy developed a greatness in Father that would not have been there otherwise.

…Father divided his time among his wives by spending a night with each one. He never missed this routine. But always before he went to bed he visited all his families, kissed all his wives and children

Photo used by permission, Sons of Utah Pioneers.

goodnight and then went to where he was spending the night. (Father was extremely affectionate.)[3]

Olive Smoot Bean ~ plural wife of J. Will Bean

There are few families to be found, where that harmony existed from the head down through all the different members of the family as existed in the family of Brother Smoot. Everyone honored Moa in her position and she in turn, honored and loved them. The children were as near and dear to her as her own, and she seemed to take as much interest in their welfare as though they were of her own flesh and blood. She was a firm believer in Celestial Marriage, and she hailed the birth of Brother Smoot's first born child, with joy and thanksgiving. She says, I was with Emily Smoot when she was confined, and when I heard the first cry of the child, my heart leaped for joy, and I loved it as my own, and as soon as it was weaned, I took it to sleep with me in my bed, and I loved it with a mother's love (her own son being grown at this time), her heart yearned for children, the want now seemed supplied, for as she says—the child walked with me when I walked, rode with me when I rode, and in fact went with me wherever I went, and I monopolized him entirely and with his mother's consent too.

The first word he spoke plainly was to call her Moa, and from that time till her death, Sister Smoot was called Moa by the whole family, and all who knew and loved her, it seemed to be an understood part that he was Moa's boy from that time on, and she took a great deal of comfort with him as the years rolled on, but that happiness was of short duration, and he was called home to a better world, without a moments warning.

…The sorrow and mourning over his death, is beyond description, those that have passed through the same ordeal, can best feel for the stricken ones. Moa's grief knew no bounds she almost refused to be comforted, forgetting in a measure that she was not his very own mother. Her grief was almost selfish in its intensity and when notified of the fact that the child had a mother, that was nearer, than herself she stood, abashed as she says, and humbled, let those who do not understand, or believe in the love existing in plural families note this fact,…it would be beyond the powers of their comprehension,…it would need the power of God to enlighten their minds, before they could comprehend it at all.[4]

Henry W. Naisbitt

In Christendom the marriage covenant is the foundation of the home. The ideas which men hold concerning it, lay at the foundation of all social order, all unity and all government, and even the welfare of future ages depends upon the theories cherished in regard to home and family associations.

…I will say as the result of my own experience, for I have lived in that relationship…it demonstrated itself to be of God, and no better time have I had in thirty years of married life than when I had three wives given me of God, and occupying but one habitation.

The power of God was in that home; the spirit of peace was there, the spirit of intelligence was there; and we had our ever present testimony that God recognized the patriarchal order, that which had been practiced by His servants ages and ages ago and revealed to us in the dispensation of the fullness of times; and although two of these have gone behind the veil, they went there with a consciousness of having done their duty in this life, and that they would meet in the life beyond those who agreed with them in practice and in faith.

From this condition came the discipline of life, the power of self-restraint, a tender regard for each others' feelings, and a sort of jealousy for each others' rights, all tempered by the consideration that relations meant to be enduring claimed more love and interest and soul than did monogamy under its best conditions.[5]

Ada Bott ~ second wife of John H. Bott

We worked together in everything we did....If any of the wives ever got sick, we nursed each other. That is how we got along....I'm never sorry about polygamy. I always said that lots of women whose husband had only one wife were not as happy as I was. My father's two wives sure did get along fine together....The wives didn't get together and talk about each other, or about their husband. I couldn't go and tell him any things on the other wives and they couldn't on me. He just said he didn't want to hear any of it. In general we all went out together, unless one of us didn't want to go. It was me who usually wanted to stay at home. I had so many children....To show you how we'd work together, take the washing. When we lived close together, we'd work together. There'd be two of us doing the washing and the third getting the dinner.

…I don't think he gave any wife more attention than any other. And as for which one he liked the most, I don't know. I used to ask him which one he thought most of and he wouldn't tell me. We wives and family were together in everything. We celebrated Christmas and his birthday's altogether, mostly at my house because I had the most room. In those days we all had fun that we made ourselves; none of your factory made amusement then like nowadays. We used to have big parties at my place. We wives just got so we loved each other's company. I just got so I felt I couldn't work alone. We all took our turns and everything went on all right.

…Yes, I believed in polygamy, and I'm satisfied with my life. I had 17 children and raised 14 of them.…I wouldn't give the experience I've had in my life for anything.[6]

Ann Agatha Walker Pratt ~ tenth wife of Parley P. Pratt

My wedding day was April 28, 1847. I married Brother Parley P. Pratt, an Apostle in the Latter-day Saint Church—a very fine man, a true and loving husband always. My husband, being in charge of the company, was extremely busy mending wagons, looking up yoke-bows, making boy-keys, or pins to hold the bows in the yokes, hunting up the cattle, mating them, finding chains, especially lock-chains, for, bear in mind there were no brakes to hold wagons back going down steep hills in those days. These and a hundred other things occupied his time. Meanwhile we were busy making and mending wagon covers and in every way aiding and assisting to prepare for the long and toilsome journey. To aid him, two of us women, which included Belinda Marden

Pratt, sixth wife of Parley P. Pratt and I, thought we would manage without his help to drive our own team, which consisted of a yoke of oxen. Belinda became the mother of six children, Nephi, the oldest one, accompanied us. At last we started and got as far as the Elk Horn River, early in June, where we camped about a month waiting for the rest to arrive, so as to organize into companies of hundreds, fifties, and tens.

In what I have written I have used the expression, "my husband" when sometimes I should have said, "our husband" for I was one of several wives, some of them as noble women as ever lived. The one I traveled and drove team with, Belinda Marden Pratt, was one of my husband's wives. A better, or more noble woman I never knew. In our traveling together we sometimes took turns—she driving one day and I the next. She had a delicate babe and when she drove I took care of it, and through all the vicissitudes of our life together we have loved and respected each other greatly and she has always been very near and dear to me and her children are next to my own.[7]

Belinda Marden Pratt ~ sixth wife of Parley P. Pratt

...I have (as you see, in all good conscience, founded on the word of God), formed a family and kindred ties, which are inexpressibly dear to me, and which I can never bring my feelings to consent to dissolve. I have a good and virtuous husband whom I love. We have four little children which are mutually and inexpressibly dear to us. And besides this my husband has seven other living wives, and one who has departed to a better world. He has in all upwards of twenty-five children. All these mothers and children are endeared to me by kindred ties, by mutual affection, by acquaintance and association; and mothers in particular, by mutual and long-continued exercises of toil, patience, long-suffering, and sisterly kindness.

We all have our imperfections in this life; but I know that these are good and worthy women, and that my husband is a good and worthy man; one who keeps the commandments of Jesus Christ, and presides in his family like an Abraham. He seeks to provide for them with all diligence; he loves them all, and seeks to comfort them and make them happy. He teaches them the commandments of Jesus Christ, and gathers them about him in the family circle to call upon his God, both morning and evening. He and his family have the confidence, esteem, good-will, and fellowship of this entire territory, and of a wide circle of acquaintances in Europe and America. He is a practical teacher of morals and religion, a promoter of general education, and at present occupies an honourable seat in the Legislative Council of this territory.[8]

Photo used by permission, Utah State Historical Society, all rights reserved.

Sarah Ellis Farnsworth Neilsen ~ daughter of Alonzo Lafayette & Eda Henrietta Tietjen Farnsworth

It was a long trail from far off Sweden, across the broad Atlantic Ocean to New York, then across the many miles to the valley of the Great Salt Lake or Zion as it was lovingly called. It took strong faith in God and a deep and abiding love for the Gospel that would give these saints from far off lands where the missionaries had found them, the courage and strength to gather in Zion. My mother, Eda Henrietta Tietjen, born April 8, 1853, and her parents, August Henry and Eda Frederica Kruger Tietjen did just that. Mother was six years old when she left her home in Sweden and arrived in Salt Lake Valley in 1859, settling first in Salt Lake, then in Santaquin, Utah.

Mother met a fine young man in Santaquin and there were prospects of a marriage but ere it could be consummated he was accidentally killed. Later she was courted by Alonzo Lafayette Farnsworth who already had two wives, Mame and Annie. He asked her to be his third wife, giving her six months in which to decide. They were married in the Endowment House in Salt Lake April 5, 1875 when mother was 22 years old....

It was sad that Aunt Mame was not given the blessing of motherhood as Aunt Annie and mother had been. So, true to the grand and glorious nobility of these two mothers, each of them offered to share their children with her. Aunt Annie to give her second son to Aunt Mame and my mother to give her second daughter to the childless Mame. Like Abraham of old, these faithful sisters put their trust in God to give them strength to do this. But it was not God who called them to suffer this great sacrifice, nor was it their husband. It was they who did it on their own, to show their love for this sister, regardless of the anguish and suffering it would cost.

In due time, when her second son Lester was born, Aunt Annie gave him to Aunt Mame for her very own. Oh what a sacrifice! When mother discovered that another little one was on the way she grew very apprehensive lest it would be a girl and her second; that she would not be strong enough to carry on with her part of this solemn pact. How she prayed to the Lord for help and the strength to do what she had promised. At this time mother was living in Tuba City, Arizona, and Aunt Mame was in Colonia Garcia, Mexico. When the little daughter was born Aunt Mame sent the name of one of her kindred whom she wanted to honor, so the baby was given the name of Sarah Ellis Farnsworth.

By the time father was ready to take mother to Mexico I was about three years old. Mother had told me from the time I could understand just what she had promised and what was to be done. As soon as she arrived in that little mountain colony of Garcia she gathered up all of my clothing and belongings and with a stout heart, heavy as lead, trembling and tearful, she took me by the hand and went to the home of Aunt Mame and laid her sacrifice of love. But good, kind-hearted Aunt Mame, who loved and appreciated mother, could not see her and the little child suffer, for I clung to mother and wept bitterly, fully sensing the great sorrow of this supreme test of love and faith. Could anything be sweeter, more God-like or more sisterly than for Aunt Mame to relieve mother of the promise she had made and was so determined to keep? Even though at times mother would faint with weakness, she never failed to fast and when blessings for which she prayed and fasted were received, she constantly thanked the Lord for them, thus setting a fine example to her children.[9]

Oluf Christian Larsen

I was born on the 8th day of April 1836, in Drammen, Norway and was baptized into the Mormon Church, April 6, 1857. After laboring as a missionary in my native land, I left home in April, 1862 to sail for the land of Zion. On April 20, 1862, I was married to Emelia Christine Olsen, a Latter-day Saint girl from my own country. We arrived in Utah, September 29, 1862; six months since we started on our journey from Norway.

…A great deal of preaching to obey the law of plural marriage by local and visiting brethren was being done by the priesthood. As we had had several young ladies staying with us and some hinting they would be pleased to live with us, we began to think that the Lord might be displeased with us if we did not embrace the opportunity which in so many ways was provided for us. It was not the lack of faith that caused us to hesitate. We knew the word of God was true and that obedience would be attended with blessings. We also realized the trials and trouble that would follow obedience. We had examples before us on every hand. We finally concluded it would not be right to shrink from duty any longer. My wife conveyed the idea to a girl working for us by the name of Amelia Anderson. She was glad and accepted the offer, so in May, 1874, we were sealed in the Endowment House in Salt Lake City. We lived together in the same house, ate at the same table and had peace and happiness in our family—even more than I had anticipated.[10]

Margaret Thompson McMears Smoot ~ first wife of Abraham Owens Smoot

With regard to the principle of plural marriage, I wish to say, that I have had experience in its practice over thirty years. I am the wife of a polygamist, I believe in the principle, and I know it to be pure and chaste; and I know that those who practice it in the spirit of the Gospel of which it is a part, are pure and virtuous. And I know, too, that purer men and women do not live upon God's footstool than those who live in this order of marriage.

I have seen the Prophet Joseph, through whom this principle was revealed; I have listened to his teachings, I have known for myself of his virtue, of his purity, of his goodness, of his desire to elevate and bless the human family, and what I say, many of you, my sisters, can bear witness of. I know, too, that virtue, and goodness, and purity, is the watchword of our brethren; I say I *know*; I do not say I believe it, but I do know for myself that what I say is true. I know it by the revelations of the Spirit of the living God—the Comforter that was promised by the

Photo used by permission, Utah State Historical Society, all rights reserved.

Savior, and it is confirmed by my long experience. I have lived now nearly seventy years on this earth, and forty-four of them have been spent serving my God in this new and everlasting covenant.

My husband, as I have intimated, is a polygamist; his other wives and his children by those are just as much a part of his family as me and mine....We have the noblest of children and the happiest of homes.[11]

Lucy Walker Kimball ~ fourth wife of Heber C. Kimball

Since 1845 I have been the wife of President Heber C. Kimball by whom I have had nine children, five sons and four daughters; have lived in the same house with other members of his family, have loved them as dearly as my own sisters, until it became necessary as our children began to grow up around us to have separate homes. Every mother has her own mode of government and as children grow in years it is more pleasant to have them under the immediate dictation of their own mother. I can truthfully state, however, that there is less room for jealousy where wives live under the same roof. They become interested in each other's welfare; they love the other's children; besides, in my experience I find the children themselves love each other as dearly as the children of one mother. In sickness, it has been a pleasure to minister to those in need of assistance.

I will say here, too, that is a grand school. You learn self control, self denial, it brings out the nobler traits of our fallen natures, and teaches us to study and subdue self, while we become acquainted with the peculiar characteristics of each other. There is a grand opportunity to improve ourselves and the lessons learned in a few years are worth the experience of a life time for this reason, that you are better prepared to make a home happy. You can easily avoid many unpleasant features of domestic life that through inexperience you otherwise are unprepared to meet.

The study of human nature is the grandest study, I can only speak for myself in this regard. When I separated from others and went to a home with my own children I placed many little safe guards around our home that experience had suggested and my children grew into their teens without having heard an unkind word between their father and mother. When the father was there everything was done necessary for his comfort—to make our home a pleasant one was the chief object of life. When absent I knew he was in good company and where he had a right to be. I stood in no fear from his associations with others, because I knew their purity of life. It is needless for me to say anything in regard to the life and character of President Heber C. Kimball. He lives in the hearts of the people called Latter Day Saints, and his acts and works are known abroad.

As time passed on he seemed to appreciate more than ever his wives and growing children. His last words to me were that he had been agreeably disappointed in my course of life, had appreciated my example as a wife and as a mother; that none had excelled me in the home life. Wherever my lot had been cast, there he had found a place of peace and rest. "Let me now thank you kindly," he said, "for every word, for every act of your life and when I am gone, which will not be but a short time, you shall be blessed and find friends." He went on to say that if he never spoke to me again I might rest assured that I had his most sanguine good feeling; his unbounded love and esteem. "What can you tell Joseph when you meet him? Cannot you say that I have been kind to you as it was possible to be under the circumstances? I know you can and am confident you will be as a mediator between me and Joseph and never enjoy any blessing he would not wish Heber to share."

These words were more precious to me than gold, as they were his last, with the addition of "I leave my peace and blessing with you, may the peace of Heber ever abide in your habitation." I do not pen these thoughts thinking that others did not share equally in his esteem, as every woman carves her own niche in her husband's affections. Heber C. Kimball was a noble whole-souled Son of God and was as capable of loving more than one woman as God Himself is capable of loving all his creations.[12]

Oluf Erickson

This was my last mission to the nations of the earth. I was thankful to God I was home again....I had nothing to mar my conscience nor take away my joy. I had honored my priesthood and my mission and found my family enjoying the same good spirit and thus we were blessed spiritually and temporally.

A few days before arriving home a great windstorm tore part of the roof off my house, but the people through their kindness replaced it

Photo used by permission, Utah State Historical Society, all rights reserved.

before I came home. I thanked God and felt to bless the people of Ephraim for their kindness and good will on my return as well as when I left for my mission. At this party I found several I had borne my testimony to in the old country among whom were Hannah and Anna Christensen to whom I preached in Copenhagen. These two I counted as the first fruits of my mission. It pleased me very much to hear that they were faithful girls. The year they had been here they had paid their own emigration as well as the emigration of two of their sisters who had come over in the fall of the year I came home.

…The leading brethren of the priesthood were advocating celestial marriage and my bishop C. C. N. Dorius told me I ought to marry either Anna or Hannah Christensen, for he said he positively knew I could get either one of them. I, myself, could also see there was nothing in the way as far as they were concerned. But I had not thought of marrying again. When considering my circumstances and conditions as they had developed and presented themselves to me and being united with the priesthood in other ways, I concluded to obey the counsel given and leave the consequences in the hands of God.…I had no trouble for my wife Maria was in perfect accord as soon as I mentioned it to her.

On the 16th of July, 1884, myself and Hannah Christensen were married in the Endowment House in Salt Lake City.…we lived in the same house, working in harmony together, each wife doing her utmost for the welfare of the household.…

The 10th of September, 1916 Anna Maria, was called home. She was the companion who shared my hardships in pioneering Circleville, where one winter the only means of getting a loaf of bread was a coffee grinder used by the community to grind a little wheat for mush and a loaf of bread. Then, also, when baby clothes were to be made for the expectant arrival, she had to use the ravelings of a piece of petticoat muslin cloth for thread to make out of her petticoat a nice white dress for her baby. That dress the neighbors borrowed when ready to have their babies blessed and named....She loved the truth and was willing to sacrifice everything she had for it when necessary. Her death was a severe loss to me....

I now moved and made my permanent home with my wife, Hannah, and her family. She is faithfully caring for me in my old age. I am now prepared to take what may follow, either good or bad. What I have done, I have done with an eye single to the will of God, and my trust is implicitly in Him. I have done nothing to harm any man and I have perfect peace in my soul. This brief sketch I dedicate to my children and to their posterity hoping they may find something in my life worth emulating.[13]

Hannah Hood Hill Romney ~ first wife of Miles P. Romney

On the 10th day of May, 1862 I was married to Miles Park Romney in the Endowment House in Salt Lake City. On the 12th day of June, in company with Thomas Taylor, my husband started on a mission to England. We had no display at our marriage, nor a very long honeymoon, but our love was for each other and we were happy in each other's society. The day we separated I felt that the only friend I had had left me. I was twenty years old when I was married and my husband was only nineteen.

In September, 1873 my husband went to Salt Lake to take another wife, Catherine Cottam, a girl of good principles and a good Latter-day

Saint. He took my oldest daughter with him. While they were gone I had part of my house finished, plastered, painted and papered. I sewed carpet rags and carried my warp and rags five blocks to the weavers to have it woven. After it was done I went after dark and carried it home. When I got home I was exhausted. The next morning I washed and dressed my little children and gave them breakfast, then sewed my carpet, tacked it on the floor, cleaned the furniture, pictures and curtains and arranged them to suit my taste, as I was very particular about my house and took great pains in having everything in "apple pie" order. I worked all day and part of the night. I had a room finished for Catherine with new carpet and furniture all ready for her.

I cannot explain how I suffered in my feelings while I was doing all this hard work, but I felt that I would do my duty, if my heart did ache....She was considerate of my feelings and good to the children. When my husband came home he appreciated what I had done. He admired the home arrangements and was surprised that I had accomplished so much in such a short time. His appreciation of my work partly took away the heartache....

If anything will make a woman's heart ache it is for her husband to take another wife, but I put my trust in my Heavenly Father and prayed and pled with him to give me strength to bear this trial; to give me a knowledge of the truth of the principle that I might be able to bear so great a trial; that I might be a support to my husband. So long as I had given my consent for him to enter into this principle I felt it was my duty to sustain him in it.[14]

Price Nelson

Speaking of his first wife Price Nelson said:

...I hadn't ever taken a girl out and she hadn't ever kept company with a boy, but we knew as soon as we saw each other that we were in love, that we had loved each other long before we ever met. Why as soon as I saw her I went over to her and took her chin in my hand and we loved each other. She said her heart jumped into her throat. God meant that we should have each other. I was a queer boy and she was a queer girl and it was meant to be. She was loyal to me all the days of her life and I was good and kind to her.

Having made a decision to enter plural marriage, Price related the following:

...I sent to Pres. John Taylor for my recommend and it was a long time a coming. Every man who got married in polygamy had to have a recommend by the bishop and have the President sign it. Well after several months it come with just J.T. signed to it. I'd talked with my wife about polygamy and she had consented. But I want to tell you it is a hard thing for a wife to have polygamy. She has to give up part of her husband's love and time and attentions to another woman and it's a great trial to her.

Well I went over to the ranch where Charlotte Ann was and somehow I forgot the recommend. I said to her father that if he doubted me, I'd let the whole thing drop, but he let me take her without seeing the recommend. We got married and I brought my wife Charlotte Ann home to my other wife. I want to tell you that my first wife has great blessings stored up in heaven for the way she lived in polygamy. She was patient and kind in everything. Down in Mexico, when I had separate homes for 'em, she would say to me, "What are you doing here? Your place is in the other home."[15]

History of Clarissa A. Cornia Putnam ~ first wife of Savannah Clark Putnam

Clara was a small, attractive girl, only five feet two inches tall and slightly built, and by the time she was sixteen she was a very popular young lady. She loved to dance and knew all the latest dances. One of her admirers was a young man by the name of Savannah Clark Putnam. Savannah was a convert to The Church of Jesus Christ of Latter-day Saints from the state of Maine. He had come to Woodruff with his friend, another convert. Later he sent for his father and mother and until their deaths, all lived in Woodruff and were active members of the Church and community.

Clara's love affair with Van, as he was always called, grew until by the time she was seventeen she decided she was ready for marriage. They came to Salt Lake City and were married at the Endowment House on May 18, 1874. When they returned to Woodruff, Clara cooked her own wedding supper to which all the adults in Woodruff were invited.

Their first home was a log cabin on a ranch on Woodruff Creek. March 23, 1875, a son was born, but he lived only a few days. They named him Clarence. It was a sad experience for Clara to see her first-born laid in a coffin and buried in the Woodruff cemetery. One year later, March 17, 1876, a second son was born. They named him Laurence Artemas. He was a strong, healthy child and the pride and joy of both his grandfathers. A year later, on April 6, 1878, they had a daughter whom they named Clara Ruth.

About this time, Van decided he should take a second wife, but this was a hard decision for Clara to make. Having only the bare necessities of life, it was difficult to think of sharing them with another wife and family. Ruth's sister, Harriet Lee, had a young woman named Anne Marie Nielsen working for her, a girl who was a convert to the Church from Copenhagen, Denmark. Van had become acquainted with her and thought she would be one who could share his life. At first Clara was sick at heart about the matter and prayed sincerely for understanding. Finally she felt that everything would work out and that Anne Marie would be a good companion for both of them.

October 12, 1878, the day before Clara's twenty-first birthday, Van and Anne Marie, or Maria, as everyone called her, were married in the Endowment House in Salt Lake City. When they returned to Woodruff, they both lived in the same home. No woman ever lived in more harmony with another than did Clara and Maria. Clara tried in every way to be a companion to Maria. Both women tried, and succeeded in making the plural marriage a success. From then on, the family had a child almost every year. Clara became the mother of eleven children; Maria had six. All but Clara's first child lived to marry and have families of their own.[16]

Rozalia Payne ~ third wife of Edward W. Payne

...I had not the slightest intention in the world of ever marrying in polygamy. I used to abhor the thought, although I think there was a fear that I might do it, for so many people did. Polygamy was not preached to us in Diaz. I won't say that it was never mentioned in the church, but it was seldom talked about and many people made fun of polygamy. I suppose I did myself. If my husband, when he asked me to marry him, had preached to me I think I should have hated it. He only told me how he would try to make me happy. And he has. Never once, not even in the darkest times, have I regretted that. I had firm faith that I was doing the best thing, and the comfort that I had then has always come to me when I was most in need of it.

I was preparing my lesson for theology at the Academy and I came across the revelation on Polygamy in the Doctrine and Covenants. I hadn't intended to read it, but I did, and when I got through I said, "I can never make fun of that doctrine again." I believed it was right, but I was popular. Girls had lots of beaus in those days and whether or not I could have, I thought I could marry any one I wished. We didn't do the courting as so many girls do now. The boys did all the seeking. When Mr. Payne asked me to marry him the family was against it. My mother didn't wish it, nor did she wish to interfere with my life. My brothers made heart breaking remarks and so did many of my friends and I suffered. For a time I didn't know what I was going to do. Mother was nearly distracted with me. But I finally felt that I was doing the right thing and that assurance has never left me.

I married with an intense desire to make a go of it. I felt that going in as I did, I should not assert myself over the other wives, that I should do the best I could and make a place for myself in the household. One woman said to me, "You get along with Lucy very well, don't you?" and I told her I'd get along if it cost me my skin. I felt that way about it.

I felt that I was living a holy principle and that I must conform my life to it. Polygamy makes people more tolerant, more understanding, and more unselfish. It gives them more contact with reality and a wider circle to love and do for. I'm not saying that, to say it has done it to me, for I can see the ways in which I have failed, but it does those things to people when they strive for it. It's not an easy way to live. We never fully conquer ourselves. And always it is the little things that makes it hard, the little foxes always upset the vines you know. It's not jealousy so much, for I had my mind made up to that, but the constant pressure or adjusting yourself to another woman. Each woman should be queen of her own home, my mother always said, and it is a natural way. We have not always had our own homes, but for the most part we have, and that has made it better. But we have been thrown closely together and each of us has irritated the other. We have our particular ways of doing things, our mannerisms, our peculiarities and in adjusting to them we have the hard times.

…There was no question of financial arrangement.…We each try to manage well as we can and to keep our expenses within a certain amount. I wouldn't want a dress if she couldn't have one and she wouldn't either. We both try to dress as well as the other and we cooperate on it.

…When one of us had illness the other has gone to help. I've spent days in Lucy's house when she needed me and she would do the same for me. Our children all have a respect for our family relations.…I have been happy in my marriage and with my children. My brothers, who were so bitter against it, admit that now. We believed in polygamy as we did in any other principle of the Church.[17]

Lucy Payne ~ second wife of Edward W. Payne

I remember one evening I was saving a seat for Rozalia. It was College Hall and I kept watching for her. When she came in she sat down by me and we kissed each other and started talking. Back of us were a boy and his parents and we heard them say, "That's two polygamist women and you can see they like each other." Afterwards we talked to the boy and learned he had been called to go on a mission. He didn't mind going but he said he knew he would be called upon to explain polygamy and he thought it such a dreadful thing that he couldn't feel to go. At first he couldn't believe that the two of us were really fond of each other and lived in harmony. After he had known us he said that now he could go on his mission with a free conscience.[18]

Mary Luella Abbott Leavitt ~ first wife of Thomas Dudley Leavitt

My husband had always told me he would marry again for he believed in the Principle. It was preached to us as strong as the Word of Wisdom and Tithing is now preached. We felt that we wanted to live as nearly right as we could and although I was of a very jealous disposition and loved my husband to distraction, when he told me his intentions of trying to live this law and asked if I could get along with his choice, I promised to try by the help of my Father in Heaven to do my best. But he knew how I loved him and how jealous I was of him. No one but my Heavenly Father knows what a struggle I had. I prayed to my Father in Heaven almost unceasingly to give me strength to live that principle and live it right.

Oct 6, 1887 my husband took me in his arms and told me he was marrying another girl but if I would be brave and stand true to him he would be true to me. Imagine me seeing him drive off with another. I knew it would never be the same. His love and time would be divided. I thought my heart would break, my throat swelled until I thought I would choke to death, but I prayed as I had never prayed before....

They were gone a week and came home about 12 O'clock at night. My three little girls in bed and a sleep. I went out in the moon light, wandered up on the hill overlooking town. I sat in the moon light and thought it out and knelt down and poured my feeling out and asked my Father in Heaven to give me courage and strength to do his will and live the law acceptable to him. It was getting late and I came home to see if my baby was alright. I couldn't go to bed, I was restless. After a while I heard them coming. He took her home and then came to our home. As he came in the door and found me crying, he stood and looked at me and I never saw him look more beautiful in his life. He was just hansom. He took me in his arms and talked to me for some time and I was so convinced the Principle was from God and I was so much relived of my Waite I was carrying. And while I knew the Lord had given it to his people and I did the best I could to live it correctly, it was a sore trial. My own heart only knows of the heartache and sorrows I passed through but now I am happy and proud to know we stood firm and true. I feel there will be a great blessing for living it through. I hope not one of the children will ever speak lightly of it or say they do not believe in the Principle because I feel it was one of

God's greatest commandments given to his people. It took courage, faith, determination and the help of the Lord to do this—with much more trust in the Lord....

We all lived together, ate at the same table, until there was 14 of us. Then we built the brick house I am living in now and intended to still live together but there were too many of us. We bought Aunt Adah a home on the same block. We never lived any further apart than that. We never had more troubles than any one family with our children. I had twelve children, 7 boys, 5 girls, lost 1 girl and Aunt Adah had 7 girls, 4 boys, all 22 living.[19]

Used by permission of David L. Zolman

Benjamin F. Johnson

The first command was to "multiply" and the Prophet taught us that dominion and power in the Great Future would be commensurate with the number of "wives, children and friends" that we inherit here, and that our mission to the earth was to organize a nuclei of Heaven, to take with us, to the increase of which there would be no end.

And while I can believe that to some plural marriage was a great cross, yet I cannot say so from my own experience, for although in times that tried men's hearts, I married seven wives, I was, blessed with the gift to love them all; and although providing for so many was attended with great labor, care and anxiety, yet there was sympathy and love as my reward. And there is not one of my children of their mothers that are not dearer to me still than life.

On my return in 1855 from a mission to the Sandwich Isles, I found that Santaquin Utah, with the homes of my family and all that I possessed to the amount of thousands, was destroyed or stolen by Indians in the Walker War, and my family homeless. And yet in 1856, although conditions appeared forbidding, council suggested that I take other wives; and feeling sure it was the voice of the Lord to me, with promise of His blessing, I married three more young wives, which was followed by cricket and locust raids to destroy nearly all our crops for five years, and yet we were neither hungry or naked.

These were days that tried the souls of both men and women, and yet the love and gratitude of any one of my children today more than repays all, and I know that both men and women in plural marriage were happy in the assurance that they were obeying the command of God and the council of His servants.[20]

Sarah Melissa Holman Johnson ~ fifth wife of Benjamin F. Johnson

I want to express my sentiments in relation to plural marriage. In it I find happiness, joy, peace, love and beauty… Six wives of us, Melissa B., Mary Ann Hale, Harriett Holman, Sarah, Susan and myself have raised our families under the same roof, having separate rooms. Children of six mothers raised in the same dooryard, most of them grown to young manhood and womanhood, are devotedly fond of each other as brothers and sisters, all of them intelligent and full of the spirit of the Gospel. We can have a dance, singing choir, theater or any social entertainment independent of any outside our own family![21]

Warren Foote

We went to see Bro. Duncan McArthur, with whom we were well acquainted. Having learned that he was one of the number who had been appointed to teach the principle of Celestial Marriage to the Saints, according to the revelation given to Joseph Smith on that subject we desired to get some correct information on that principle. The doctrine having never been taught publicly, there were all sorts of reports concerning it. He very willingly taught and explained to us that doctrine in such a simple manner, as to remove all prejudice we had against the doctrine of plural marriage. He showed us the necessity of marriage for eternity in order to obtain an exaltation in the Celestial Kingdom.

I felt to rejoice, that the doubts and fears that had been resting on my mind with regard to plural marriage caused by the traditions of the Fathers, were all removed. By the aid of the light of the Spirit, I could in a measure see the glory and beauty of that principle. It was very plain that our marriage covenants were only for time, they last only through this life. We are not bound as husbands and wives for eternity but all our domestic relations were dissolved at death. We learned that the celestial law binds for time and eternity, and our connection as husbands and wives, parents, and children never ceases in time nor all eternity, and we will continue to increase while eternities roll around. We went and looked at the Temple and in the afternoon started for home. Went four miles south of Nauvoo and stayed over night at Bro. E. Hanks.[22]

Joseph C. Bentley

…When I asked Maggie to marry me I told her that I wanted her to know I might some day take a plural wife and she said, "I wouldn't think much of you if you didn't." Polygamy was one of the greatest Principles ever given to our Church. By it men could rise to greater heights than they could without it, but we were not able to live it and it was taken from us. It is a true principle and someday when we are able to live it, it will be restored. I wanted to marry in polygamy because I considered it a great privilege and blessing. My family were able to live it because of the unselfishness of my first wife. She stood by me in everything and helped all of us to live happily. Without her cooperation I could not have done it. When my second wife died she took her family and raised it as her own. Now my first two wives are dead and I have Mrs. Bentley to care for me and to make a home for the children when they wish to return home.

…Her children say that the second wife was somewhat spoiled, but that there was little friction and the two women lived harmoniously. Maggie made it a practice as long as Gladys lived to visit her for a moment each night and to kiss her goodnight. During the day they might have occasional words or one may have hurt the other's feelings, but the goodnight kiss was one of understanding. Neither woman asked pardon of the other, but it was understood that all grievances were forgotten and the day started with no hangovers from yesterday….[23]

Helen Mar Whitney ~ plural wife of Horace K. Whitney

My husband was advised by my father to take another wife. He studied my feelings and took one whom he had cause to believe loved me and my children, and would cause me the least trouble. She lived with me in the same house till she had three children, and had it not been for this, and the care of my own little ones, we should never have separated. It was more agreeable to her to remain, as we had lived kindly together. Mr. Whitney has built her a large, comfortable house within a few feet of mine, and has deeded to each of us our homes. Our children have always lived more peaceably than many who had one mother. I am called "Aunt" by them and their mother is called the same by my children. When visited by my relatives from the east, and from California, I have invited her to make their acquaintance. One was the husband of a cousin who passed through here on his way east. He wrote a letter to his wife, telling all about what he had seen; and the other wife and children coming in and out of my house and being at my table. Said he, "I have looked at both their faces but can discover no nail marks."[24]

Phoebe Woodruff~ first wife of Wilford Woodruff

I was brought up to regard strictly the principles of morality; and when the order of Celestial Marriage was introduced into the church, I thought it the most heinous thing I ever heard of, and I opposed it to the utmost of my power, thinking I was doing right. But I began to consider and reflect, and I learned that it came through the prophet of God. I regarded it in an earnest light, and therefore I went to God my Heavenly Father, and inquired of him of the truth of this doctrine. He made it manifest to me as plainly as I could have wished, that it was of Him, and that it came as a principle of salvation to the women of this generation. If I am proud of anything in this world it is that I accepted the principle of plural marriage, and remained among the people called "Mormons" and am numbered with them to-day.[25]

Jens Iver Jensen

October 24, 1883—I married Inger Anna Christensen which was in perilous times to enter plural marriage, but I realized the time had come for me to be obedient to that principle, and I did so in honesty of heart, fully knowing I was to obey that principle now or never. I felt that I would be under condemnation for disobedience. I have passed through many hardships and trials because of it, but now in the evening of my life I testify to the truth of the law that it is of God and has given me valuable experience. I have no regrets for being obedient to this law but feel grateful to God who gave me strength to obey and feel the Lord has blessed and sustained me in it.[26]

Story of Emma Louise Elliker Wood ~ second wife of Sam Wood

Emma Elliker became the second wife in the Wood family. Born in Beaver on the 21st day of January 1862, she was nine years younger than the first wife, to whom she was ever after a beloved sister....Aunt Jody and Aunt Emma made it their business to love each other. They were devoted sisters, companions, sharing each other's joys and sorrows.

What a formidable introduction this to the dignified and all requiring realm of plural marriage, both for Miss Elliker of Beaver and for the first wife who had accepted her wholeheartedly as Sister Emma. If they had not drawn without reservation together, they would have flown violently and forever apart. To be initiated through all this tribulation without permitting the cold, the weariness, privation and general discomfort to sour them one against the other is proof beyond challenge that they were women of superior faith and purpose. This was to be proved many times in the hectic years ahead. I must affirm from my personal observation of these women to the end of their lives that they adapted themselves to the demands of every trying occasion with most unusual efficiency.

Mutual love and harmony prevailed with all of them from the first; that is the chief phase of this life performance which makes it interesting to contemplate. Whether it was duty that begot love, or love that begot duty, we may not know. Possibly their good works are the kind that may always be expected when love and duty meet. We do know that love was legitimately born, that it was par excellent in quality, that it remained untarnished and shining to the end.

Of Emma it is affirmed by those who knew, "She lived twenty-five years in plural marriage and never had so much as one unpleasant word with the first wife. Their children mingled freely together at mealtime and at bedtime; mutual love and respect prevailed in the whole family; not two families, but one."[27]

John S. Stucki

When I was a single young man, I used to think because I was so bashful that I would never dare ask anyone to have me; and then after my humble, secret prayers, how wonderfully my dear wife Barbara Baumann was led to me…and then my dear wife Karolina Heimberg; and then again how very wonderfully my dear wife Louise Reichen was led to me through heavenly dreams, in answer to her and my secret prayers, with all of who I could have a happy life.

As I have had my prayers heard and answered many times, so also can you all have your humble, secret prayers heard and answered, with blessings upon your heads, our dear children and children's children, under like faithfulness, even to the latest generations, for it pleaseth the Lord to have His children draw near unto Him by keeping His commandments, and in humble, secret prayer.

Never allow yourselves to become weak or neglectful in the service of the Lord and to mankind. Always remain true and faithful to the end. The race is not to the swift, nor the battle to the strong, but only to those who hold out faithful in their service to God, faithful to the end of their lives, that will gain eternal life, which is the greatest gift of God which we can gain unto ourselves only through continuous living up to the requirements of the Gospel and of those that are placed over us in the Holy Priesthood of God.

I wish to exhort you all to pray to God to bless you in all your undertakings; whether you go on a trip or whether you go to plant your crops. Ask His blessings upon the planted seed and ask Him to inspire you how to take the best care of it. If you buy a new wagon or machine, ask the Lord to bless them for the best good, that you might not have any bad luck while using them. If you get a new suit of clothes, ask His blessing upon it.

Especially in making a choice of a companion for life and all eternity, which is one of the most important things, you do need to pray to your Heavenly Father, for then I believe that He will lead you to some good soul with whom you can have a right happy life forever, as I, after praying to the Lord in sincere and humble secret prayers, have had good souls led to me through heavenly manifestations; with whom I have had a very peaceful, happy life. Better companions in every way I could never have wished for—with whom I expect I will have a happy meeting on the other side never more to part.

It is my firm belief, that as I have had my humble, secret prayers heard and answered that He will hear and answer yours likewise; and also lead you to good companions with whom you can have happy lives.[28]

Bathsheba Wilson Bigler Smith ~ first wife of George A. Smith

Being thoroughly convinced, as well as my husband, that the doctrine of plurality of wives was from God, and having a fixed determination to attain to Celestial glory, I felt to embrace the whole Gospel, and that it was for my husband's exaltation that he should obey the revelation on Celestial Marriage, that he might attain to kingdoms, thrones, principalities and powers, firmly believing that I should participate with him in all his blessings, glory and honor.

Accordingly within the last year, like Sarah of old, I had given to my husband five wives; good, virtuous, honorable young women. This gave them all homes with us, being proud of my husband and loving him very much, knowing him to be a man of God and believing he would not love them less because he loved me more. I had joy in having a testimony that what I had done was acceptable to my Father in Heaven.[29]

Chapter Five

A Righteous Posterity

"A reward that he with his four wives will receive here and hereafter will depend on us, his children, his sons and daughters, grandsons and granddaughters, and all of our descendants."[1]

~ *Louis Orson Brandley*

As church members became established in the west, they left behind a life of tribulation, sacrifice and sorrow. An important part of this history, is the sacrifice of Saints who established the principle of plural marriage. It is because of these individuals that the promised blessings of Abraham are available to their posterity. For in serving the Lord they have served us, by leaving not only a great heritage but also their testimonies of truth and strength for us to build upon.

Each individual had challenges to meet and crosses to bear, but through their adversities came a conviction and testimony of the divine purpose of plural marriage. Continuing through their children and grandchildren, there remains a true devotion, love and respect for those who shared this wonderful experience in their lives. From the prolific writings of these early Saints came heartfelt recollections of the past along with prayerful hopes for the future—a testimony and promise of *more than one*.

Celestia Snow Gardner ~ daughter of William Snow

Courtesy of LDS Church Historical Department

My father, William Snow, was a humble, faithful man and was acquainted with the Prophet Joseph Smith. He loved him dearly. When Joseph taught the principle of plural marriage, father took a second wife, Sally Adams, and was married to her in the Nauvoo temple. Soon after this the Saints were driven from Nauvoo, and father's second wife went with her father's family to Council Bluffs. In leaving Nauvoo, the first wife, Liddie Levitt, died of exposure, leaving two little girls. When father and his two motherless children reached Council Bluffs, his second wife joined him and took care of his family. He remained in Council Bluffs for two years, as each man was required to save enough grain to plant in the land toward which they were bound. In 1850, a company was organized to start for Utah. Brother Snow was made captain of the company. In this company was a young widow, Maria Wines, who had three sons. My father became acquainted with her, and after arriving in the valley, they were married. A few years later he married another widow, Anna Rogers, a lone girl whose sisters had died on the plains.

We called the second wife Aunt Sally. She was a most perfect woman. We lived in a duplex house in Pine Valley—Aunt Sally with her six girls and one boy, and mother with her six boys and two girls.

In the evening we would all gather in the backyard and play together, pomp, hide-and-seek, ante-aye-over, and other games. We seldom quarreled. We used to remark that our big family had fewer difficulties than the family where there was one mother and one set of children.

After we were older, father built another home for Aunt Sally, and remodeled the duplex for mother. During this time father moved Aunt Maria to Pine Valley from Lehi, where we had all lived in earlier days. Soon after father was elected county judge, he needed a home in the county seat at St. George, so he moved Aunt Roxanna from Lehi to St. George. Now all his families were in southern Utah.

One strong factor in helping us get along so splendidly was that we all kept busy. The girls knit stockings, and helped with the sewing. Aunt Sally's oldest girl used to spin and weave. We younger ones helped to card the wool bats to put in quilts. I would take my knitting and run into Aunt Sally's or Aunt Maria's, of an afternoon. We did not like to knit alone. We were always neighborly, running back and forth into each other's homes. When we put on a quilt, all the girls of the family would help. The boys hauled the wood, plowed fields, planted and harvested the crops. So we were a busy and happy family.[2]

Rose Durrant Ostler ~ daughter of John & Elizabeth Jane Ginger Durrant

My remembrance of Auntie (father's first wife), is a very sweet one. She was kind and thoughtful of us and we were taught to be mindful of her. It was a pleasure to be so, because she returned every kind act so graciously. For instance, she always stayed up late at night reading or doing beautiful handwork, so in the morning before I was allowed to practice my music on the organ, I would rap gently at her door to see if the music would annoy her. Generally she would tell me that she loved to hear me practice. She was a splendid musician and always encouraged me to play.

Our house was a large double one. I remember each spring and fall, we would ask Auntie which side she preferred, and changed accordingly. She was subject to sick headaches and would pull the shade at the window when she was resting. We were taught to walk quietly by her window. These things were not a trial to us. And now in looking back to those years, I would not ask for it to be different. Our lives are richer for having her live with us and the lessons we learned are priceless to us now.

My own mother, Elizabeth Jane Ginger Durrant, was the second wife of John Durrant. When she was staying at her brother's home in Salt Lake City, my father and his first wife came to visit. A friendship developed between the family and this young girl, which resulted in her marriage to Mr. Durrant. Of her association with the first wife my mother wrote, "Sister Jemima and myself lived together nearly all our married lives, under the same roof, with separate apartments. We have endured many trials, but through it all we were blessed. We never allowed our tongues to wound each other. We nursed and administered to each other and through all our weaknesses our great desires were to live according to the principle we had been privileged to enjoy. Aunt Jemima passed away, August 2, after a faithful life's service in the Church of God. My life has been enriched through her fellowship and I hope to prove worthy to meet her."

My mother's life was one of sacrifice, but not only did she lay up treasures in heaven, but found happiness in the work of every day. Both of these mothers were busy women, in the homes and serving their Church. Both were ready to make happy the members of the family.

Possibly the following words written by my mother will prove this statement: "Dear Auntie (Aunt Jemima), enjoyed the blessing of raising our fourth son, Joseph Smith Durrant, until her death. On Friday, December 12, 1886, while washing and dressing the baby, a spirit rested on me and made it clear to me, Aunt Jemima was to take him as her own, and as if he had been born to her." He was nineteen years old when Auntie passed away.

There was a third mother in our family, but because she lived farther away, I did not know her so well, but I remember whenever I went to her home she always gave me something especially nice. Her children and mother's boys and girls are all one big family of brothers and sisters.[3]

Elizabeth Hayward ~ daughter of Phillip & Martha Roach Pugsley

I never remember that when going to Aunt Clarissa's home was not like going to my own home. I was the eldest daughter of the family, therefore it oft-times happened that I was called to my aunt's to tend the smaller children. Father's tannery and gristmill was near her home, so we were there a great part of the time. Her home was like our own. There was always harmony between the wives and children.

When my mother died, Aunt Clarissa maintained she had lost her best friend. So near to each other were the daughters of our family that people did not know who were the mothers of the different girls.

All through our lives their joys were our joys and their sorrows were our sorrows.[4]

Daughter of Thomas Chamberlain

Father was always very desirous that there never be any ill feelings between his wives and children. One wife remarked to a friend, "Tommy won't allow us to hold feelings." What a wonderful training to be able to school ones-self to straighten out and erase any misunderstanding before it came to sufficient proportions to cause trouble. He desired his children to always greet each other with a kiss, making no difference if they did not belong to the same mother.

Imagine if you can, six women in love with one man, and living in peace and harmony with each other. One little incident will show the wives' sisterly feelings for each other. Their home equipment and utensils were very meager. It was necessary for several of them to use the same utensils, such as washtubs, boilers, etc. One morning Ann decided to wash. She arose early and put her water on to heat, and was ready to put it over the clothes when Ella's girl came over. Not knowing that her Aunt Ann was planning on using the utensils, she asked for them, saying her mother wanted to wash. Quickly Ann emptied the water and gave the waiting girl the things she had come for. When Ann was criticized, by an observer, for what she had done: put off her work for

Photo used by permission, Utah State Historical Society, all rights reserved.

someone else, she quietly remarked, "I can wash tomorrow, it might not be convenient for Ella to wait."

Father put responsibility upon his boys early and always expected them to do their best. One son said, "I would rather make a mistake before anyone than father, not that I fear criticism from him, but he always expects me to do the best I can." He liked to keep the children busy and sometimes said he would rather have his children dig post holes and fill them up again than be idle. He was very desirous of having everything neat and orderly about the place and when not busy with the farm or other work, he kept fences and machinery in neat repair. He drove a span of black horses which he always kept trim and shiny.

Father was a great believer in education. He never had much opportunity himself to attend school, but after he was married he hired a man to teach him at nights. After a busy day at his work he would apply himself diligently to his studies, and became an educated man. In later years he bought a home in Provo and moved one of his wives there to keep a home for the young people so they could attend the BYU.

…Father was always a companion to his children. Always solicitous of the welfare of each one. I wonder how the days and nights were long enough for him to do all he did, and give each such personal attention. He was a real father to his sons' wives and daughters' husbands, taking them whole-heartedly into the family He was very proud of his large family. He was ordained a Patriarch in 1896, being one of the youngest Patriarchs in the church at the time. He served in many public offices of trust and honor from the time he was 19 until his death. In all his work he was noted for his thoroughness and honesty. He was wise in counsel and was often arbiter in difficult situations. He was devoted to his church and to his public duties and was always willing to sacrifice his own interests when duty called him to help him.

Father had had six faithful wives, Elinor A. Hoyt, Laura Fackerell, Ann and Ellen A. Carling, Chastie E. Covington, and Mary E. Woolley. They bore him fifty-five children. At the time of his death, March 17, 1918, he was sixty-three years of age, and had living five wives, forty children, ninety-four grandchildren, and one great grandchild.

There were twelve pair of twins in the family, one hundred sixteen have served their country in military service, sixty-six have filled foreign missions, and six gave their lives in World War II. Members of the family have served a total of one hundred forty-seven years as missionaries for the L.D.S. Church in addition to stake missions. Hundreds of combined years have been spent in other church positions. Among the family there have been numerous bishops, several stake presidents, and officers in every other calling in the stake and wards.[5]

Mary Viola Allred Stout ~ daughter of Byron Harvey Allred, Sr.

I feel my father was a great and noble man, honest and obedient to all tenets of Mormonism, therefore worthy to be numbered in the archives of the pioneer history. Too often only the stories of those who reach the top in leadership are preserved, while those loyal to this leadership, doing the fulfilling and being responsible for the success of a given project, are forgotten.

In those early days of Mormonism the law of Plural Marriage had been given to the Saints....It was most difficult and took people of the highest caliber to obey it worthily. Only the most obedient, unselfish, were able. Father entered the law of plural marriage by taking a wife, Matilda Rolf. She gave to father his greatest increase, bearing him eleven children.

As our Book of Mormon states, this practice of polygamy was "an abomination in my sight, unless I command it, to raise up a righteous seed." The Lord had given this commandment, the church needed "a righteous seed" to get the church on its feet, with stalwart leadership. It was given for this reason. The leadership of our church today attests to this, as the majority of our present leaders are descendants of those who obeyed this principle. Like any other principle, this too was abused. Always man's weakness manifests itself by the way he obeys or disobeys authority.

As history records show, the law of plural marriage met with much opposition, not only from without but within the church. Those who strove to obey it were persecuted, ridiculed, and even accused of immorality. There were doubtless some who took advantage of its privileges to "co-habit" but I am sure the majority of men were of the highest moral caliber, obeying it only because it was commanded.

Those who fortunately chose women obedient, submissive and charitable enjoyed a relationship of the highest order. Those men who relished the license, of course, soon found their households one of confusion, jealousy, and retaliations. I guess the Lord appreciated the first group and tolerated the 2nd group to the limit of his endurance.

It was about the year 1904 when an apostle of the church visited the conference in those Mormon settlements and proclaimed a new and final Manifesto to the effect that henceforth no more plural marriages were to be consummated in all the church, anywhere. It had run its course, fulfilled its destiny, at least for the time being. Many arose in a spirit of rebellion, unwilling to obey those in authority and thus the seeds of apostasy were sown.

My father, ever obedient, even though not comprehending fully, accepted the verdict of those in authority over him. He may have on various occasions wondered why it had been so strongly and emphatically preached, then withdrawn but he acquitted. This is the duty of all true Saints. Ours not to reason why! Obedience is the first law of heaven and it must ever be thus, to maintain order. That all members could accept this truism! How much trouble, bitterness, disobedience, apostasy, cutting off, could be avoided. If only people were willing to be obedient to those whom God places at the head. Two of Father's children and many of their families refused to accept the edict of the church and soon separated themselves from the church. Thus our family had divided itself. Not of one fold, one shepherd. I'm glad Father left us before all this took place.

Father left a family that at once became divided as to locality and all too soon became divided as to beliefs. If only his posterity could have remembered his example to remain steadfast and true and obedient always to those who preside in the church of God as restored in these last days. What egotism makes men think the church leaders are wrong because they think differently than themselves? As was asked of Joseph Smith one time "What would happen if these people would not sustain you?" Joseph Smith answered, "Then the Lord would raise up people who would." So likewise in these days—many turn away and fall by the wayside, but the Lord has always raised up others who will sustain the Prophet who stands at the head of His church.

Father was one who did this and always would. May we, his descendants, emulate his example and be worthy to meet this tall, kindly, every loving father who gave us his good name, unmarred by rebellion but ever obedient to Divine authority.[6]

Daughter of John Bowen

Mother and Aunt Hannah always got along. I can't remember anything differently. Aunt Hannah liked children and she used to play with us and help us more that Mother did. We had right good times when we were children. Aunt Hannah would teach us dialogues and little plays and on holidays we would give programs. On Christmas we nearly broke our necks to see which one would get to the other house first. On holidays we always had our dinners together. One holiday Father gave us all a dime and on our way to town my half brother swallowed his. We divided with him. I can remember seeing Father going up the aisle of the Church with one wife on either side. He took them both to all public places. He said where one went the other must go too.

He used to spend a night each at the places. He would eat supper, breakfast, dinner, then go to the other house. But he was back and forth all day long. Each of the wives had a garden and cows and pigs and chickens. The farm was in common and both families had equal shares from each. We each had our flour bins. When Father would come back from his trips he would bring each family a big bag of candy. He would bring two sacks of flour and sometimes two bolts of cloth. The cloth would be about the same kind but a little different in design and color. When Mother needed a new stove, he bought her one. Aunt Hannah had a good stove, but he bought her a new picket fence in front of her house. Their houses were close together, with no fence in between,...⁷

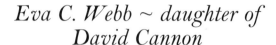

Eva C. Webb ~ daughter of David Cannon

We were more fortunate than most families because in place of one mother we had three, any one of whom would give her all for any child in the family, and no sacrifice was too great for them to make for each other. In 1859, father (David Cannon), married "Aunt Willie," his first wife, eight years after this in 1867, with her consent he married "Aunt Joe," and took her to share the home with him and his first wife. For ten years they lived together as sisters, never a cross word between them.

In 1877, "Aunt Rhoda," the third wife, was brought to this home. She was welcomed by the other wives and introduced to the children as another mother who had come to live with them. This attitude was kept during all our lives, and we learned through all the years that they were indeed mothers to us all. Once "Aunt Joe" and "Aunt Rhoda" had babies so near the same age, the latter nursed both babies, the former had to feed hers artificially.

By 1880 the family had increased in numbers until it was necessary to have more room, so father bought another place and "Aunt Joe" and "Aunt Rhoda" were moved into the new home. Here they lived, until again the family needed larger quarters, then the third home was provided. Each did the part of the work she liked best to do. "Aunt Joe" always milked the cow and did other outside work, while "Aunt Rhoda" did the dishwashing and other house work. Washing, ironing and sewing they did together. The older children helped whichever mother needed them. We went from one home to the other freely and were always welcomed by the mother.

There were quarrels between us children, but no different than those between own brothers and sisters. This was largely due to the justice of our father. He was so absolutely just in his treatment of our mothers and their children, there was never a tinge of jealousy in the family. A more just man never embraced the principle of plurality of wives. When he went on a trip the mother who went with him left her children at home knowing they would be cared for as if she were there.

I well remember when Walter was eight years of age he had to undergo a major operation. "Aunt Rhoda," his mother, was not able to go to the hospital with him, so "Aunt Willie" left her children at home and took him to Salt Lake and stayed those weeks until he was able to come home, just as devoted as if he were her own.

When Raymond was a small boy he had to have a serious operation on his leg. His mother took him to the doctor at Cedar City and stayed as long as necessary. But after her return they had to take him back for treatment. If "Aunt Joe" could not go with him, "Aunt Rhoda" did, and his mother knew he would be taken just as good care of as if she were there.

When the last call came to "Aunt Joe," her only wish was that they send for "Aunt Rhoda," who was living in Hurricane. As long as she was conscious she kept asking how long before "Aunt Rhoda" would be there. So you see the friendship of their youth maintained through all the years. These two wives were at the bedside of "Aunt Willie" when the final summons came to her, and they sincerely mourned her passing as she had been a true and unselfish friend to them to the very last.[8]

Leah Rees Reeder & Margaret Rees White ~ daughters of John D. & Zillah M. Rees

There were no special preparations when father was to spend his week at our house. We were all very glad to see him and had a good time when he was there, but nothing special was done. He came on Monday morning. He kept his best clothes at Aunt Mary's, and all his work clothes at Mother's. On Sundays, when he was staying at our house, he went to Aunt Mary's in the evening and changed his clothes and then came back and spent the night at our house. His laundry was done wherever he happened to be, and so was his sewing. He had to have lots of work clothes because he was a blacksmith.

Family prayers were said night and morning. When father was around he led, and the wives led when he was not there. Father was a mild-tempered man. I don't know what it was that used to make us <u>want</u> to do everything he said for us to do, but we never misbehaved.

The children played together all the time they could. But they didn't eat meals away from home. Father didn't encourage that, just as he wouldn't have encouraged his children to eat at any other person's home. When we went to Aunt Mary's to play, we always told her how long Mother had said we could stay, and she always sent us home when the time came. It was the same at our house.

I can remember yet the time Aunt Mary got the melodeon organ. No, there was never any discussion about to which house the organ should go. Aunt Mary's girls were older, and it went there. We all knew we could take lessons on it, and go up and practice. We never thought to question where the organ should go.

We girls often were sent to help with housework at the other house. Father would come in and say "Mary needs you today" and that is all there is to it. We went. And Father sometimes varied his routine of where he spent his time. I can remember when Aunt Mary's children were ill. Father must have been over there during the day because I heard him and Mother talking about it. Later Mother said, "John, I'm sure Mary needs you tonight with those sick children. Suppose you go over there and stay tonight."

[*Speaking of third wife*] I remember now how quickly we loved Aunt Cecelia and Lorenzo [*son*]. She was a beautiful woman with snappy dark eyes and black hair. We were so very glad that Father had married Aunt Cecelia. For a while she lived with Aunt Mary, until he built her a house a block or two from the shop. She fitted into the picture exactly, and Father just added another week onto his schedule and went on as before.[9]

Margaret Smith Watson ~ daughter of Orson & Caroline Maria Carpenter Smith

Orson Smith, a native of England, emigrated to Utah in 1853, locating first at Farmington, later made Logan his home....At this time he met Caroline Mariah Carpenter, a talented young convert from Putnam, Connecticut. The incident of the first meeting of Orson and Carrie is related by Orson in the following words:

"Near where the stake house now stands, Carrie was driving a cow that had strayed from home. She wore a sun-bonnet and when she lifted her head, I saw the loveliest face, and something said to me, 'some day she will be your wife.' I laughed at the thought. I was so different from her, but the thought came true. Our meeting ripened into the most congenial attachment which finally was consummated in marriage."

Three months after their marriage, Orson was called to Paradise, to preside over the ward. They took up their new duties, with love for the work and devotion to the cause of truth. Carrie was called to be the first president of the Y.L.M.I.A. of Paradise, by Eliza R. Snow. It was in Mutual that she met the two young girls who later became her companions in marriage.

Sarah Ann Obray...Annie, as she was called, was a sweet devoted girl,...Annie was married to Orson Smith, October 1879, in the Endowment House. She was welcomed into the family home where the wives lived happily and reared their children together. Strangers visiting the family could not tell which was the mother of the various children. They loved each other dearly, even more than sisters....They shared each other's joys and sorrows. July 4, 1884, another young girl, Mary Ellen Wright, came into this family....

The three families lived in separate homes, but the lots were joined together. Orson provided all sorts of sports and amusements for his 27 children, and they had their pleasures in the home. He spent a week with each family, but never a night did he retire without visiting each family, having prayers with them, and kissing all good night. Often a family meeting was held where different members of the family took part on the program. Instruction, council and advice were given those present. There was no gossip. If a child was chastised, it was never in the presence of another. There was no doubt differences of opinion among that trinity of mothers, however the children grew up without that knowledge.

Three months before Carrie's death, she called her oldest daughter to her and said, "If you have ever seen in me anything contrary to the spirit of love for Auntie, or for Aunt Mary, it is of the head and not of the heart."[10]

…To make a success of polygamy, I think the wives have got to love each other better than they love their husband. Father's wives were like that. Before mother even came to Utah she was thoroughly converted to the Gospel and plural marriage. She said that a woman who had been able to marry a fine, upright man ought to be willing to share him with other women who might marry him.[11]

Descendant of Margaret Forquhar Cruickshank Morrison

In 1893, upon the occasion of what would have been the 50th wedding anniversary of Grandmother and Grandfather Morrison had he lived another four years, the entire family including all the children of the subsequent wives as well as her own, gathered together to honor and show their love and respect for Margaret F. C. Morrison. Because of this demonstration, Grandmother wrote the following and read it to all who were assembled that day.

> My dear Children, In response to your good feelings manifested towards me this day, I must confess that I am too full to give expression to my feelings as I should like. In reviewing the past fifty years of my life it brings many things to my mind, but the one of greatest importance to me is that since I embraced the Gospel I have been enabled by the help of my Father in Heaven to prove faithful to my Covenants which I made at the waters of baptism, and in the House of the Lord.
>
> In looking upon your faces, all so happy and cheerful today, I feel thankful that I never once opposed my husband in his wishes to enter into the order of plural marriage. We all know that it was a great trial, but we have stood it and will receive our reward.
>
> Our Husband and Father is absent in body, but I believe he is present in spirit, watching over our doings this day with great interest, mingled with joy and pride, to witness those of his family who are here so united in their efforts to make one heart glad.
>
> May God help us to live in the future so that when our mission here is ended, we shall all meet in one grand family reunion that shall be lasting as eternity is the heartfelt prayer of—Grandma M. F. C. Morrison.

Grandmother remained in the adobe cottage named by her, Bon Accord, which means "unity", until her death in January 1910.[12]

Agnes Melissa Stevens Wilson ~ second wife of Guy C. Wilson

We celebrated Marguerite's 7th birthday, all together July 24, picnicking at Wandemere Park. It was Utah's Pioneer Day, a state holiday. Throngs of people sought the shade of the huge trees to picnic on the grass. Children crowded around every swing, slide and teeter-totter but the Guy C. Wilson family, papa and both "mamma-girls" with the nine children, altogether, found a secluded spot where we felt completely secure—we were strangers among strangers....

He [*Brother Wilson*] wanted the children to grow up in close association with each other. He would tolerate no evasions. The children were to be continually assured of his pride in them, and in their mothers. Each child was to be nurtured in an atmosphere of pride in their parentage, an atmosphere so charged with loyalty, respect, and love for one another that offense of the sanctity of our family relationship would be as natural to them as the air they breathed....

He had carried out instructions from his fine leaders, to the best of his ability, step by step. He had been assured of their trust and confidence as well as faith that he would receive a special blessing. Now he was grateful for the actual, literal realization of that blessing. His paramount purpose and desire was to have his children grow up together, to have his family stand beside him, chin up, heads high with pride, confident of the future.

Brother Wilson's emphasis on a close, intimate, harmonious relationship between the two groups of children was steadily maintained throughout his life, and more especially through their impressionable early years, as long as they were within the sheltered family circle. His warm, affectionate, fatherly influence, and his understanding and sympathetic wisdom, yielded guidance, protection and inspiration, as his children matured and met life's major problems. The children were nurtured from infancy in affectionate consideration and loyalty for each other, and for their respective mother and auntie in each case. Patience, Consideration, Cooperation were three Wilson's Watch-Words in our dedication toward the goal of united perfect harmony in this Divinely Inspired Order of Marriage.[13]

Elizabeth T. Blair ~ daughter of Charles Alphonzo & Sarah Hammond Terry

My father, Charles Alphonzo Terry, was born in Otsego, Cortland Co., New York. He with his father's family moved to Michigan, in which state they received the Gospel in May, 1843. He crossed the plains in 1850, settling in Union, Salt Lake Co. Here he with his brothers engaged in farming. Charles also labored as a cooper. He and his brother, Lysander, met and loved two sisters, Fanny and Phylinda Loverige. After a romantic courtship Phylinda became the wife of my father, Charles Terry, while Fanny married his brother.

My father and his wife were very happy. Three children were born to them. Their first sorrow was the death of a child. The mother never recovered from the shock of losing the little one, and from that time on her health failed. Her husband sought assistance at the home of a neighbor, John Hammond, securing the services of his twenty-year-old daughter, Sarah. She entered the home, taking the full responsibility. Sarah took a mother's interest in the children. As time rolled on the mother knew that she was not long for this earth and was fearful of the future of her babes. So with her full consent Charles Terry married Sarah Hammond, June 23, 1857. Shortly afterward the first wife died, but Sarah had already gained the love of all members of the family. Sarah, my mother, taught the girls all the domestic arts of the pioneer home. During their early married life they were called as pioneers to St. George. All through these years of hardships, my sweet, patient mother stood bravely by my father, helping him in every way she could, encouraging him in his manual labor and the work he was called upon to do for his Church. She was the mother of twelve children, six of them dying in childhood.

In 1871, father married as his third wife, Emeline Wilson. She lived in her home which father built for her. It was on the same lot as ours. She proved to be a worthy wife, always willing to help in any family project. Because she, like my mother, was a very prayerful woman, blessed with an abundance of patience, the family grew to love her. Aunt Emeline was an excellent homemaker and a good cook. At this time mother was not very strong, so to make her life more pleasant, Aunt Emeline would cook delicious dinners and invite our family to dine with her. When mother was unable to walk the distance to her home, she and father's oldest daughter, Cyntha, would carry her over in a chair. Oh, how delicious these meals were to us all. She was so unselfish. We all shared her home.

After mother's death, Aunt Emeline came to live in our home and took the mother's responsibility. There were times when I was rebellious, feeling I was misunderstood, but her love, her forgiving spirit so completely won me, that all our grievances were forgotten. I remember how I worked for fifty cents a week and with my meager wages bought us each a dress of the same pattern. How happy we both were.

She proved a great blessing to our home, standing bravely by father in his declining years. It was she who nursed and cared for him during his last sickness.

After father's death she would come to my home and make me her confidant, and my life was happier because of her. I nursed her during her illness and helped prepare her body for its last resting place. She was a true mother to us all.[14]

Jennie Cowan Iverson ~ daughter of William Cowan

My father, William Cowan, emigrated to America in 1851, with his father's family. On reaching St. Louis, they found their money was about gone, so they lived there for two years, preparing for their journey to Utah. Here he met his future wife, Mary Brown. They crossed the plains in the same company, and at the end of the journey they were married, settling in the Eighth Ward. One evening they attended a dance in the old meeting house, where they were introduced to Jane Stoner, a charming English girl. A friendship developed between these people that was to last a life time, for on March 30, 1867, Jane became the second wife of Mr. Cowan. All parties concerned knew they were breaking no law, for at that time there was no law in the United States against plural marriage. Mr. Cowan took the new wife to the family home where she was received as a real member of the group. Being a splendid seamstress, she sewed for the entire family. The night before I was born she stayed up part of the night to make a new suit for one of my half-brothers.

Soon Mr. Cowan built an addition to the home in which the new mother raised her family. The first wife, although the mother of five children, took care of the second wife at the time of the birth of her eight children. The children loved both mothers. Perhaps the real devotion of these mothers was shown at the time of illness in the family. At one time my mother's two children, Minnie and Albert, were taken ill with diphtheria. Our other mother came into our house, where she nursed and fought for the lives of these children until death came, then she helped prepare the bodies for burial.

After my other mother's children had married, she lived with her daughter Agnes Romel. But when she was ill, her first wish was, "Call Jane." During her last illness no one could ease the tired body, no one could bathe her, dress her, as well as Jane. Her last request was that mother prepare her body for its final resting place. When death came, mother said, "her best friend and loved one had left her." I loved the children of this other mother, as I loved the children of my own mother. She made my life richer, better,...[15]

Mary Reiser Gallacher ~ daughter of Henry & Magdalena Schneider Reiser

In 1862 my father, Henry Reiser, watchmaker and jeweler, purchased a piece of property from Brigham Young, 12fi x 20 rods at the corner of Third West and Fourth South, just opposite the old Fort, now Pioneer Park. Here he built three homes to house his families, totaling sixteen children living at one time. In these three homes were three different mothers, each a queen in her own domain and each loved and honored by the children of the other homes almost as much as by her own.

Courtesy of LDS Church Historical Department

Each mother had a different personality. Perhaps that made Aunt Catherine's and Aunt Margaret's such fine places to visit and to play, and the fact that all of us were exactly on the same basis as brothers and sisters, the only difference being, we slept and ate our regular meals with and asked permission for favors from our own mothers. One big happy family in one big yard, neatly foot-pathed to each back door. Did I say yard? No, it was a lovely garden of flowers at the front of each home. Lilac bushes and violets, tulips and bleeding hearts, ribbon grass and the old-fashioned Sweet William and Sweet Rockets grew in profusion. Beds of vegetable gardens bordered with all kinds of currant bushes, gooseberry bushes, raspberry bed, rhubarb patches. Fruit trees of every description were planted in the orchards, not forgetting the big, black walnut trees that provided many happy evenings before the old stone hearth on cold winter nights in our old-fashioned kitchens of the early days. Even the sidewalks outside the rods of whitewashed fences were shaded by the graceful foliage of black and white and purple mulberry trees.

There were also spaced between the gardens, huge lucern patches. What fun to play hide-and-seek behind the big piles of sweet smelling new mown hay, and among the trees in the early evening before time to study and retire. Each mother gladly divided her store from her own garden with the other two. And each mother gladly taught her arts to all the children. How well I remember when I was but ten years old, Aunt Margaret taught me to knit a pretty pattern of cotton lace, speaking in German, and paid me for embroidering a little baby dress. She was a refined, gifted musician, and as I sewed under her big apple tree she sometimes sang and played her guitar. You see, her father was a music-master of the Old Heidelberg school. My mother was of a literary inclination and a student, and Aunt Catherine a fine seamstress and cook and of a radiant and happy disposition.

From my earliest memory a birthday was the occasion for ten pounds of Z.C.M.I. hardtack to be given to me to divide with all the others proportionately, being only three in my home, six in one and seven in the other, we each enjoyed the same amount. We gave no other gifts on birthdays and expected none except from our own mothers. Sixteen children meant plenty of candy all the year 'round as well as on all the holidays—Decoration day and Christmas, the Fourth and Twenty-fourth of July, and Thanksgiving time, and even Washington's birthday. You see, father knew we had a sweet tooth.

Unity and harmony prevailed, for father always played fair with us all and taught us all to do the same with each other. There were three girls, Sidonia, Aunt Catherine's oldest daughter; Alice, Aunt Margaret's eldest child, and I, one from each home born within eighteen months, who were inseparable. People often commented on the lovely companionship we three enjoyed all our lives. We were in the same classes in the old Sixth Ward School and in Sunday School. Hand in hand we went with father on Sunday afternoon to the Tabernacle and to concerts in the Ward House. Later we sang in the Tabernacle Choir together. How dearly we loved each other! No jealousy existed, only sincere admiration. All these women were of Swiss descent, as also was my father. We are proud of our freeborn Swiss heritage.

We three girls were each given the same sort of Christmas gift, yet different enough to be personal, also dress patterns, ginghams for school wear, white muslins for Sunday and the Twenty-fourth, and wool linseys for winter time. Did one need new shoes for Sunday, each had them. In our clothing the personality of the mother again shone forth, and our tastes were cultivated. Father came into each home long enough for family prayers. Mother took charge of morning prayers. Every Sunday morning father called in each home to remind us of Sunday School at ten o'clock. When we had a grievance, he brought us together to settle it and to listen to both sides impartially.

Each child was given one year of advanced education, and according to our different tastes, we advanced or learned some trade. I took up dressmaking. Four of Aunt Margaret's daughters are university women and fine teachers. Two are business college graduates. Two of mother's children are university students, following music, dramatics, and public speaking. The fault was our own if we failed. Father encouraged university work by lending the money to be repaid later when one earned. Over and above everything we were taught honesty, and to love our religion and all its blessings. We were told that the best doctors and the best lawyers were always the cheapest. Death had taken nine in early childhood, so a healthy body and mind were to us the best assets.

We never knew what debt meant. We were provided liberally with the necessaries of life, purchased in wholesale quantities, and each home received a certain allowance weekly. When we were small, father fed and cared for two cows himself, cutting his own lucern in early morning hours for exercise, then washed and dressed for breakfast and family prayers, and was off to work at 7:30 a.m.

Each wife had her own coop for her own chickens and could follow her own inclinations for her personal income. In Aunt Margaret's home eventually there were seven living daughters, trained to do their part so well that even the four-year-old could use dust pan and brush up the crumbs that might fall from the table, and those just older would wash and dry and put away the dishes, scouring knives and forks and tins. The others helped with the bedroom work. So at nine a.m., invariably all the children over six years of age were off to school and the mother would sit sewing and mending stockings while the baby played at her feet. All were taught never to put away clothing until well brushed and mended. Stocking darning was taught as soon as one could hold a needle and a stocking with a ball inside.

Aunt Catherine had a son and daughter. Sidonia became her mother's dependable, loving companion in the home, and there were three more boys and a little girl later. Syd, as we called her, was immaculate in person and lovely to look upon with as fine a personality as one could ever meet. She, too, mothered the younger boys, who at early years were taught trades, and two of them are still in places of business, where they entered forty years or more. Fine sons of a fine mother and father, honored and successful citizens.

Every phase of healthy, happy childhood these wonderful mothers and our understanding father provided….Eleven children of different parentage were taken into our homes at different times and kept until their parents arrived here from across the sea. Could anyone ask for richer or fuller childhood days or finer companionship between parent and child?…

Today in the prime of life, and the old age of some, all of his children are enjoying the fruits of his labors and the beautiful memories of our loving mothers, and fine father. God bless them.[16]

Susan Ellen Johnson Martineau ~ Granddaughter of Ezekiel & Julia Johnson

It was in Ramus that Joseph taught my father [*Joel Hills Johnson*] and grandmother, Julia Hills Johnson, the principle of plural marriage, both of whom accepted it. When I was but a child, I had a positive testimony that Joseph was a Prophet of God, and as I looked at him he seemed to me like a heavenly being. And at the age of eighteen I had a positive testimony that the principle of plural marriage as revealed through Joseph was a pure and holy one. In conclusion I declare myself a living witness to the fact that Joseph Smith the Prophet not only taught but also practiced plural marriage, anyone to the contrary notwithstanding.[17]

Eva Jenson Olsen ~ daughter of Andrew Jenson

In June 1885, a mother and two young daughters left the shores of England to migrate to Utah. The two girls had joined the Latter-day Saints' Church but the mother still belonged to the Church of England, but accepted the Gospel shortly after her arrival in Utah. This little family arrived in Salt Lake City on July 7, 1885, and after visiting with relatives and friends in Fort Herriman for a short time, settled on Second West Street, between North Temple and First North. It was not long before Emma, the eldest of the two girls, contracted typhoid fever and she became so sick that her life was despaired of. It so happened that Andrew Jenson, who is now the Assistant Church Historian, lived just two doors north of the family and in a neighborly way, called at the home to enquire how Emma was getting along. He was asked to administer to her, and she was almost instantly healed under his administration. A courtship began and although Brother Jenson had a wife and four small children, it was not long before he asked Emma to be his wife. They were married in December 1886, and in January 1887, the first wife passed away, leaving the father with these four small children.

Emma who had been a "lady's maid" in England, had practically no experience in taking care of a home or children, and hence, this new responsibility was quite a hardship for her. But her mother and sister, Bertha, often came to her home and helped her with the housework, cooking, sewing, etc. The mother was an expert seamstress and Bertha, who had been a nurse to the children of a doctor in the small town of Steyning, England, proved very helpful in caring for the four motherless children. No wonder that Brother Jenson saw the virtues of this younger girl, and decided to ask her to be his wife. She consented, and so it happened that this mother and two daughters who had left England together were never separated, but lived as one family as long as their lives were spared.

Photo used by permission, Utah State Historical Society, all rights reserved.

Emma became the mother of three children, two boys and one girl. Bertha has one son. All were reared together, living in the same house, and it can truthfully be said that the children scarcely knew which was their own mother. Bertha had always loved children very dearly and seemed to have a natural instinct in caring for them. She was the one who bathed and dressed the children when they were small, and she was never happy unless she was doing something worthwhile for them. Emma, on the other hand, loved the social part of life and fitted in perfectly along this line. She was never happier than when she was entertaining her friends.

Many emigrants from the old country lived in the Jenson home until they were able to make a home for themselves. Emma passed away in April 1937, and while her children loved her dearly and deeply regret that their mother is gone, yet they still have a second mother in their Aunt Bertha, who is always ready and willing to lend them a helping hand. They can go to her for advice and counsel. She is also a great comfort to her husband, who is nearly 87 years of age, and the children are all happy in knowing that their father has a wife still living to add joy and comfort to him during his remaining days on this earth.[18]

Alean Ellison Layton ~ granddaughter of George D. & Elizabeth Golightly Watt

The question is often asked, "How did the wives of a polygamist get along?" It seems that the wives of George D. Watt, lived in perfect harmony together, everything being divided equally among them. When the three wives lived together in Salt Lake City each woman would take her turn at doing the cooking and all kitchen and dining-room work, while the other two wives would take care of the washing and all other tasks as needed to be done for their families. The clothes would be sorted out as they came from the wash and each wife would do the ironing for her own family.

When the Watt family moved to what was called Kaysville but is now Layton, Elizabeth and Alice each had rooms by themselves as Alice was becoming old and Elizabeth had her husbands mother living with her. Sarah and Martha lived together for a time but when their families enlarged each was given a section of the house for herself and family. All these sections consisting of three or four rooms each were under the same roof. The groceries were bought in bulk and each woman was given a portion according to the number in her family. Never at any time was there any serious trouble among them. Then as the children came to Elizabeth, Sarah and Martha, they were taught to live together as one large, congenial family.[19]

Vivian Parkinson Taylor Hales ~ daughter of Samuel R. & Charlotte Smart Parkinson

...Samuel, [*Samuel Rose Parkinson*] was born in Barrowford, Lancaster, England, on April 12, 1831. His family came to America in 1848 where he joined the church and came to Utah in 1854, settling in Kaysville. His first wife, Arabella Ann Chandler, born 1824, was sealed to him in 1855. They moved to Franklin, Idaho, in 1860 at the request of the General Authorities to colonize the area.

After moving to Franklin he married sisters as his second and third wives: Charlotte Smart (born 1849), in 1866 and Maria Smart (born 1851), in 1868. As of April 12, 1964, descendants of Abrabella and her nine children totaled 989, of Charlotte and her ten children 655, and of Maria and her thirteen children 461, for a total posterity for Samuel and his three wives of 2,105 souls.

Courtesy of LDS Church Historical Department

Today I want tell you some of the things about my father, so you will know about your Grandfather Parkinson. He was a great pioneer and colonizer. When he was young he had dark curly hair, but when I knew him his hair was gray and he was quite bald headed. He was 63 when I was born so I didn't see the dark hair, only in pictures. He had all his teeth but one when he died at 89. He had a gold cap on one of his back teeth that showed when he had a hearty laugh. He carried a toothbrush in his inside coat pocket, "to use when necessary," he said. He weighed about 170 pounds. He wore a beard and whiskers and he looked a bit like his son, Samuel.

When Father was going with his first wife there in St. Louis that's where they heard Mormonism. They were close to a family named Clement's and they told Father about Mormonism. Well, Father believed it. He says to his bride to be, "You know, I know that's true, that church. And if I join it I'm going to join it whole hand or none. And that means if there ever comes a time I think I should take another wife I'm going to do it." That's what he said to her before she was married to Father. And so it wouldn't do for me to say that she didn't come to the church as much as he did. She wasn't quite so sure about it.

But anyway she did join the church, and Father did have that in mind all the time.

…Father thought so much of me. I was the last child of thirty-two, and he took me everywhere he went. I remember going to Preston, oh, we went up there once or twice a week in the buggy, and I had a little box that yeast came in, just a little one that I could sit down on the bottom of the buggy. And I'd sit on that and Father would drive the horses.…

I don't remember my father disciplining me at all. But I know when I'd go out for parties and things, and when I first started going with boys a little bit when I was about sixteen, if I'd come home and we'd stand on the porch a little while like they do, Mother would come out and she'd say, "Vivian, your father's walking the floor." That's all she'd have to say. We were supposed to be in at ten o'clock every night unless it was some big dance or something like that.

They did have responsibility, but believe me Father was the one that was head of the house. He had the priesthood, of course, and that was the head of the house. But they discussed things among themselves.…I think they were just as happily married as anybody could be. When I'd go up to Aunt Maria's, the third wife, I would see the same thing. I'd go up there lots of times to play with Glen, my brother, and he'd come down to our place to play.

…And then I'm so glad that I was a polygamist child, you just can't know. Because I believe it so thoroughly, and we were taught to do it, you know, to be in it. The polygamists we had to be nice to all of them, they're all our brothers and sisters.

...Father said it takes a good man to live polygamy, they have to be. They've got to be fair and honest or you can see there'd be trouble all the time....He had many friends, mostly that were a polygamist like he was, because they had so much in common. Father was honest and fair with every business dealing he ever had. One of his sayings was "Let your word be as good as your bond." He was cheerful and happy. He wouldn't allow any quarreling or bickering among his family. And it takes a firm, honest man to live in polygamy and make a success of it, and this was one of his main qualities.

Oh my, I wouldn't change polygamy for the world. I'm so happy that I'm a polygamist child. I don't think people are quite good enough to do it now.[20]

Susa Young Gates ~ daughter of Brigham & Lucy Bigelow Young

Long ago in the lovely vales of Utah, dwelt a childless married woman. After seven years of unsatisfied longing, loving and reverencing her worthy husband more as the years proved him of the highest type of manhood combined with great integrity, they both greatly desired offspring which it seemed in vain to hope for.

At last, with full consent of all concerned, this worthy man took to wife another Daughter of Zion, familiarly known and loved by both husband and wife. In a year's time a son was born to gladden their hearts and in due time another son, then a daughter, then another son.

Then after nearly a score of years of waiting, a son previously named and promised by the spirit of prophecy, came to the childless wife. She was visited by hundreds of women, rejoicing that she had triumphed and saying she had been blessed even as Sarah of old, she herself knowing it was even so. And with such foundation they felt they must not fail.... Their greatest ambition being to prove worthy to live in this most holy and revealed family order, with the father of their offspring throughout a never ending eternity.

The writer having been born through this same order of marriage, her father one of the first apostles in the church, cannot do otherwise than revere the same.... With her belief and remembering her pioneer parents, feeling a divine assurance that these conditions will exist forever in eternity for the faithful, she naturally enters a plea for the principle as a Souvenir for her children, this pure and holy order born in.[21]

Daughter-in-law of
John Ezra & Phoebe Ann Covington Pace

Phoebe Ann Covington Pace was born, November 21, 1857, in Big Cottonwood, and was married to John Ezra Pace, January 11, 1877. This was the second marriage of Mr. Pace. His first wife was Caddie Ivins, who passed away six years after his second marriage, leaving four children under eight years of age. By that time Phoebe had three children of her own, but she tenderly mothered the seven children all

Photo used by permission, Utah State Historical Society, all rights reserved.

under eight years of age. As time went on, nine more children were born to her. Her duties and labors were many.

Fifteen years after the death of his first wife, Brother Pace married the sister of Caddie, whose name was Julia M. Ivins, and to her were born three children. When her baby was three months old she passed away and left besides the tiny baby, two daughters of the ages of four and six. To the sixteen children Phoebe was so tenderly mothering were added these three and for the second time she experienced mothering a band of little tots. This time there were five babies under three years of age and eight under seven years. She not only raised these nineteen children, but she gave every one a mother's care and love. She lived to be 73 years of age.

…I have been in the family since her youngest child was three years old and I know of her sincere, beautiful and sacrificing mission.[22]

Sarah Ellis Farnsworth Neilsen ~ daughter of Alonzo Lafayette & Eda Henrietta Tietjen Farnsworth

It takes those of extra strong character, of great integrity, deep and abiding faith in God and a lasting love, to live the law of plural marriage. It takes lives of unselfishness, patience, faith, understanding and a strong determination to succeed in this, as mother did in all things. For her the price was not too high. She loved the truth and the gospel above all else.[23]

Part Two

A Promise for Tomorrow

Chapter Six

A DIVINE PURPOSE

"I wondered and still do, if there was ever any principle or doctrine or plan following that had so acutely affected the lives of good people, either for happiness or anguish, or satisfaction, or sorrow,..."[1]
~ *Agnes M. Wilson ~ plural wife*

It is the primary purpose of the Lord "*...to bring to pass the immortality and eternal life of man.*"[2] This is accomplished in part by the marriage of man and woman as first instituted by the Lord in the Garden of Eden. It was here that Adam and Eve, being the first of the human family on earth, entered into this sacred covenant. This union was essential for the eternal progression of Adam and Eve as they could not obtain exaltation without each other. This was made apparent by one of our most noted prophets, Joseph F. Smith, as he defines this requirement.

> Men and women may be saved singly, but men and women will not be exalted separately. They must be bound together in that union which has been revealed in this great latter dispensation. The man is not without the woman in the Lord, and neither is the woman without the man in the Lord. Whatever men and women may say or think in

relation to this, they cannot obtain an exaltation in the kingdom of God single and alone....[3]

Although salvation is a gift to all mankind, the glory of eternal life and exaltation is reserved for only those who meet the requirements. These requirements include celestial marriage, a union that seals a man and woman for time and eternity by one in authority. Heavenly messengers gave this authority to the Prophet Joseph Smith (see D&C 110:13-16), when the Church was first organized, and it has been handed down by divine succession to each prophet since that day. Only those individuals holding the priesthood, who have been given the authority by the laying on of hands, are able to seal a man and woman for eternity.

In addition to this requirement, there exists another aspect of the marriage covenant needed to enter into the highest kingdom of heaven—the principle of plural marriage. This requirement, which is part of the new and everlasting covenant of marriage, is essential for all who obtain the highest degree of glory as indicated in D&C 132:4 wherein it states: "*For behold, I reveal unto you a new and an everlasting covenant;* [plural marriage] *and if ye abide not that covenant, then are ye damned; for no one can reject this covenant and be permitted to enter into my glory.*" As part of the revelation given on celestial marriage, this particular scripture stands as one of the most important doctrines of the Church.

Speaking on this important subject again, President Joseph F. Smith explained with great certainty that a monogamous marriage (a man married to just one woman), is not sufficient to obtain the fullness of the celestial kingdom:

Some people have supposed that the doctrine of plural marriage was a sort of superfluity, or non-essential to the salvation or exaltation of mankind. In other words, some of the Saints have said, and believe, that a man with one wife, sealed to him by the authority of the Priesthood for time and eternity, will receive an exaltation as great and glorious, if he is faithful, as he possibly could with more than one. I want here to enter my solemn protest against this idea, for I know it is false....

The marriage of one woman to a man for time and eternity by the sealing power, according to the law of God, is a fulfillment of the celestial law of marriage in part—and is good so far as it goes—and so far as a man abides these conditions of the law, he will receive his reward therefor, and this reward, or blessing, he could not obtain on any other grounds or conditions. But this is only the beginning of the law, not the whole of it.

Therefore, whoever has imagined that he could obtain the fullness of the blessings pertaining to this celestial law, by complying with only a portion of its conditions, has deceived himself. He cannot do it.[4]

Whether we are commanded in this life or the next, the Lord has made it clear that participation in plural marriage will be a requirement for those seeking exaltation in the celestial kingdom. This may require a change in thinking for millions of members in the LDS Church who feel that living a righteous life in monogamy is sufficient.

In addition to the promise of eternal exaltation there remains an even greater purpose in the practice of this principle—the ability of church members to provide earthly tabernacles for the many spirits in heaven. Not only did this circumvent Satan's efforts to stop the growth of the Church, but it also gave those special children of our Heavenly Father the opportunity to be raised by parents committed to the teachings of Jesus Christ.

It was a considerable challenge for many members as they realized the sacred responsibility and eternal consequences of bringing children into the world and raising them in the gospel. One devoted mother and plural wife, Hannah Simmons Gibb, an early Latter-day Saint, received a personal witness of plural marriage. In her autobiography she not only recalls her spiritual experience but also shares her testimony of motherhood.

> When I was twenty-one, the Relief Society asked a girl friend and I to go stay with a sick woman one night. She was one of Joseph Smith's wives and had been a widow many years. She kept us getting her up and down all night. Then she straightened out and was so still I thought she had passed away. She lay that way for quite a while. Then all of a sudden she sat up, and looking at me said, "The Lord has chosen and called you to go into plural marriage." I said, "Not me, but my friend." She said, "Yes, you, and you ought to be thankful for the privilege of living the highest law of marriage." She died that same day.
>
> I thought a lot about what she had said for I had always said I would not marry a man who would not live plural marriage, but I wanted to be the first wife. But the Lord ordered it otherwise. I had had many chances of marriage but none suited me.
>
> One year a family came from England and lived next door to us. They lived there two years. They were good people but very poor. The man and his wife seemed to take a liking to me. The Bishop gave him what work he could, and I noticed he was always first to pay

donations when the Bishop asked for something for the church. He was a first class shoemaker and he worked at his trade all he could. He was called to lead the singing for church and Sunday school. He also taught singing classes. He and his wife wanted me to marry him, but I refused, as I had always said I would never marry a shoemaker or an Englishman.

I was ready to leave for Salt Lake City to stay, intending to go the next morning. That night I was awakened, hearing a voice calling me. I answered and the voice said, "You are called to go into plural marriage and, if you know of the good work you have to perform in a short time, you would not put it off any longer." I decided then, if it were the Lord's will, I had better marry this man.

Early the next morning our neighbor and his wife came over, saying that during the night they had a manifestation that they should get their endowments and take me with them. We all thought we had better take heed and do the will of the Lord. The Lord had said that all must obey to whom this principle was made known. Therefore, Brother and Sister Gibb and their five children and myself went to the endowment house where they had their endowments and sealings and I was married to him.

Hannah recalls later in her journal…

One time when I was hanging out my washing, I said to myself: "I guess I am good for nothing but to take care of little children." Right beside me I heard a voice say, "Do you not know that if you teach your children and bring them up acceptable before the Lord you will accomplish one of the greatest works a woman ever performed on the earth?" I said, "With the help of the Lord, I will do the best I can."⁵

Illustration by Randall Gibb, used by permission, all rights reserved.

The gift of motherhood is one of the greatest blessings the Lord can bestow upon his daughters. It is through this great honor that spirit children waiting in heaven are provided with earthly tabernacles and raised to maturity in the loving arms of a mother. How great this joy is multiplied in the practice of plural marriage, each child having more than one mother figure to attend to its spiritual, emotional, and physical needs. And each mother can enjoy the blessings of her own children as well as the others with whom she shares her heart and possibly her home.

It was the design of our Heavenly Father that through plural marriage many of the spirit children waiting in heaven would be sent to families reflecting the teachings of the Savior. For this reason, early

Church leaders encouraged husbands and wives to participate in this divine principle, with an understanding that they were co-creators with our Heavenly Father. It was through this process that the most choice and noble spirits of heaven, those who were held back until this time of restoration, would come to earth. Addressing some of the early saints, Orson Pratt in 1852 declared:

> I have already told you that the spirits of men and women, all had a previous existence, thousands of years ago, in the heavens, in the presence of God; and I have already told you that among them are many spirits that are more noble, more intelligent than others, that were called the great and mighty ones, reserved until the dispensation of the fullness of times, to come forth upon the face of the earth, through a noble parentage that shall train their young and tender minds in the truths of eternity, that they may grow up in the Lord and be strong in the power of His might; be clothed upon with His glory; be filled with exceeding great faith that the visions of eternity may be opened to their minds; that they may be Prophets, Priests, and Kings to the Most High God.
>
> Do you believe, says one, that they are reserved until the last dispensation, for such a noble purpose? Yes; and among the Saints is the most likely place for these spirits to take their tabernacles—through a just and righteous parentage. They are to be sent to that people that are the most righteous of any other people upon the earth; there to be trained up properly, according to their nobility and intelligence, and

Photo used by permission, Utah State Historical Society, all rights reserved.

according to the laws which the Lord ordained before they were born. This is the reason why the Lord is sending them here, brethren and sisters; they are appointed to come and take their bodies here, that in their generations they may be raised up among the righteous.[6]

This admonishment was heard not only in the early days of the Church, but in our day as well, as latter-day prophets continue in their efforts to fulfill the Lord's plan. Urging the sisters in the Church to recognize their role of motherhood and increase their posterity, the Prophet Spencer W. Kimball extended this call: *"Come home, wives, to your children, born and unborn. Wrap the motherly cloak about you and, unembarrassed, help in a major role to create the bodies for the immortal souls who anxiously await."*[7] President Joseph Fielding Smith has also given counsel on this matter. Speaking to both husbands and wives about their responsibility to bring children into the world, he gave this admonition:

> When a man and a woman are married and they agree, or covenant, to limit their offspring to two or three, and practice devices to accomplish this purpose, they are guilty of iniquity which eventually must be punished. Unfortunately this evil doctrine is being taught as a virtue by many people who consider themselves cultured and highly educated. It has even crept in among members of the Church and has been advocated in some of the classes within the Church.
>
> It should be understood definitely that this kind of doctrine is not only not advocated by the authorities of the Church, but also is condemned by them as wickedness in the sight of the Lord.[8]

It should be clear to us that providing earthly tabernacles for spirit children is an important part of our earthly duty and a crucial part of the Lord's plan. The principle of plural marriage still stands as one of the most effective ways to accomplish this responsibility as evidenced by early church members who righteously accepted this call. Because of their obedience and devotion to the Lord, plural families were able to bring many children into the world. It was not uncommon for each wife in a plural family to have 8 to 12 children, thereby fulfilling the Lord's divine purpose in "raising up a righteous seed."

As indicated many times in the journals and writings of early Latter-day Saints, plural marriage was not an easy doctrine to accept and practice. Not only did it require a great deal of spiritual strength but patience, tolerance, and compassion as well. Through the challenges that plural marriage brought forth, came a fulfillment in part of the Lord's plan to build a strong and righteous people. This was spoken of in Doctrine & Covenants 136:31: *"My people must be tried in all things, that they may be prepared to receive the glory that I have for them, even the glory of Zion; and he that will not bear chastisement is not worthy of my kingdom."*

Many of the saints recognized that their personal trials were a fulfillment of the Lord's purpose. An early member of the Church and plural wife, Jane C. R. Hindley, expressed her understanding of this in her journal:

> My husband came home last night, I don't see him as often as I could wish, but his business and "other" things prevent it, and as I am a sincere believer in plural marriage; I do not wish to murmur.

> I have lived in the order of Celestial Marriage 28 years. I have not been without my trials in the practice of this principle, but I have had peace and comfort, and I have had sorrow, I expected to be tried.
>
> I entered into it, with that "expectation", I had my prejudices to subdue, my selfishness to overcome and many things to contend with, but the Lord has said that he would have a tried people.[9]

While many encouraged their husbands to enter into plural marriage and would even choose their sister-wives, not all found it easy to share their eternal companion. Nor did giving their permission as required, relieve the anguish felt by many entering this covenant. The stark reality of their husband sharing affections with another woman, was a challenge that many had to overcome as expressed by one plural wife.

> ...However, it was not until after school closed for the summer that the dread hour came. My husband seemed especially tender that day and as twilight approached, especially attentive to baby Elizabeth. After lingering over the evening meal, for some reason we both arose, drawn together impulsively standing in the dining room near baby E. asleep in her baby buggy, when suddenly he took me in his arms and said, "I'll not be back this evening my treasure." I felt the blood drain from my face. He held me tightly for a few minutes while I pulled myself together and said, "This is the hour I have been steeling myself to face, but with our baby Elizabeth, I will be alright."[10]

From the very beginning the Lord knew what would build character and strengthen members of his Church. Through various latter-day prophets he would institute many doctrinal principles which the Saints would be compelled to follow, such as tithing, the word of wisdom and the law of consecration to mention a few. These principles provided the Saints, in addition to the obvious physical and spiritual blessings, a strong base to build a unique culture that would set them apart from the world and establish them as the Lord's chosen people. Certainly the practice of plural marriage was one of the most challenging gospel principles the saints had to accept. An early historian for the Church, B.H. Roberts, describes in detail the position of the Saints in relationship to plural marriage and their understanding of its purpose, consequences, and eternal blessings. In his published six-volume work, *Comprehensive History of the Church*, he concluded:

> Latter-day Saints did not accept into their faith and practice the plural wife system idea that it would increase the comfort, or added to the ease of any one. From the first it was known that it would involve sacrifice, to make a large demand upon the faith, patience, hope, and charity of all who should attempt to carry out its requirements. Its introduction was not a call to ease or pleasure, but to religious duty; it was not an invitation to self-indulgence, but to self-conquest; its purpose was not earth-happiness, but earth-life discipline, undertaken in the interest of special advantages for succeeding generations of men. That purpose was to give to succeeding generations a superior fatherhood and motherhood, by enlarging the opportunities of men of high character, moral integrity, and spiritual development to become in larger measure the progenitors of the race. To give to women of like character and development a special opportunity to consecrate themselves to the high mission of motherhood. The new and everlasting covenant of marriage, was instituted for the fullness of God's glory.[11]

In this cause was the Lord's purpose carried out. The Church grew in large numbers fulfilling the prophecies of restoration and blessing not only this great nation, but the world as a whole. Today we find the posterity of those who participated in plural marriage in all walks of life—doctors, lawyers, engineers, political leaders, entrepreneurs, and presidents of vast corporations, as well as many noted individuals who have excelled in service to their fellow men.

These are the individuals who today share in the blessings of past obedience, for it was the promise to all who abided by the "new and everlasting covenant" or plurality of wives, that their blessings would be great as that of Abraham. And so the Lord has said, *"This promise is yours also, because ye are of Abraham, and the promise was made to Abraham; and by this law are the continuation of the works of my Father, wherein he glorifieth himself"* (D&C 132:31). As we look at the brothers and sisters who sacrificed so much to further the work of the Lord, we find the promised blessings securely established in their posterity. For in serving the Lord they have served us by leaving not only a great heritage, but their testimonies of truth and strength—a legacy of *more than one.*

Chapter Seven

NO MORE CHILDREN

> *...with us the basic aim and divine purpose of marriage, either plural or single, is children; next to eternal salvation the most precious of all the blessings our Heavenly Father has to bestow upon His sons and daughters.*[1]
>
> ~ *Elder A. Milton Musser*

We are born into the world as spirit children of our Heavenly Father, having taken those necessary steps to insure our free agency in this life by the decisions we made in our pre-mortal life. It was there in the pre-existence as spirit children that we observed, considered and decided for ourselves which cause we would support—the plan of Lucifer or the plan of Jesus Christ. The Prophet Joseph Smith described this incident: "*So the devil rose up in rebellion against God, and was cast down, with all who put up their heads* [stood] *for him.*"[2]

In the war in heaven there was no middle ground or fence sitters. All spirits were compelled to decide for themselves whom they would follow. In the end, our Father in Heaven wept, as did many others, for the third that chose to follow Satan. For they were cast out of heaven to this earthly place to continue their existence without the privilege of a mortal body. Joseph F. Smith shares his perspective of these events:

We were there. We sang together with the heavenly host for joy when the foundations of the earth were laid, and when the plan of our existence upon this earth and redemption were mapped out. We were there; we were interested, and we took a part in this great preparation. We were unquestionably present in those councils when that wonderful circumstance occurred when Satan offered himself as a savior of the world if he could but receive the honor and glory of the Father for doing it. But Jesus said, "Father, thy will be done, and the glory be thine forever." Wherefore, because Satan rebelled against God, and sought to destroy the agency of man, the Father rejected him and he was cast out, but Jesus was accepted.

We were, no doubt, there, and took part in all those scenes, we were vitally concerned in the carrying out of these great plans and purposes, we understood them, and it was for our sakes they were decreed, and are to be consummated. These spirits have been coming to this earth to take upon them tabernacles, that they might become like unto Jesus Christ, being "formed in his likeness and image," from the morn of creation until now, and will continue until the winding up scene, until the spirits who were destined to come to this world shall have come and accomplished their mission in the flesh.[3]

It is essential in the completion of the Lord's plan that all spirit children designated for this earth life fulfill their mission by obtaining a body before the Savior returns. In an effort to thwart this plan and extend his rule upon the earth, Lucifer has rallied his forces,

Photo used by permission, Utah State Historical Society, all rights reserved.

commanding all that would follow him to fight against those who would provide this opportunity.

Many of the early saints were aware of this evil and fought the battle both in word and deed. With great faith and conviction, they stepped forward and embraced the principle of plural marriage to protect the sanctity of the family and provide righteous homes for the countless spirit children waiting in heaven. Helen Mar Whitney, plural wife and mother, expressed these views:

> Polygamy, at different periods, has been practiced as a corrector of evils and a promoter of purity; because of the wickedness and corruption into which the world has sunk; and this is the present condition of all civilized nations. Every sign goes to show that we are nearing the end—the winding up scene which all the ancient prophets have foretold, as well as the Prophet Joseph Smith. It was revealed to the latter that there were thousands of spirits, yet unborn, who were anxiously waiting for the privilege of coming down to take tabernacles of flesh, that their glory might be complete.
>
> This, Lucifer and his armies, who were cast out of heaven down upon this planet, have been doing their utmost to prevent. Their greatest punishment is in not having bodies; and their mission is to throw dust in the eyes of the children of men, that they may not see the truths of heaven. It is through Lucifer's wicked schemes that so many thousands of tabernacles have been and are being destroyed and thereby those choice spirits have been hindered from coming into this state of existence, which event is of the greatest importance to them.[4]

For the Saints who practiced plural marriage, bringing children into the world was not only a commandment but a way to combat the efforts of the adversary. They clearly understood, perhaps better than we do today, the importance of providing earthly tabernacles for the millions of waiting spirits. They also understood that the battle in heaven did not end with Satan being cast out, but continues here upon the earth as he pursues his goal of unrighteousness—to tempt, overcome and destroy all that would further the plan of the Savior. From the early days of the Church to the present time, the battle goes on as our Church leaders continue to warn us of the adversary's goal. From the insight of Bishop Victor L. Brown comes this description of Lucifer's plan:

> At the present time, there are wars and rumors of wars. Yet, may I suggest that there is another war currently going on in the world—a war more destructive than any armed conflict—yes, a war between good and evil, between freedom and slavery, between the Savior and Satan.
>
> Satan's legions are many. In their battle to enslave mankind, they use weapons such as selfishness; dishonesty; corruption; sexual impurity, be it adultery, fornication, or homosexuality; pornography; permissiveness; drugs; and many others. I believe Satan's ultimate goal is to destroy the family, because if he would destroy the family, he will not just have won the battle; he will have won the war.[5]

Speaking on the family, President Spencer W. Kimball offers this warning, "...*the evil one knows where to attack. He is going to attack the home. He is going to try to destroy the family.*"[6] One only has to look at the cause to understand the effect. The following data is compelling and stands as a witness to the effective efforts of "the third of heaven" who work on Satan's behalf. Elder Richard P. Lindsay, speaking at the annual "Celebration of Families Conference," painted this dismal picture:

> When compared with other developed countries, our country has one of the highest divorce rates in the world, the highest teenage pregnancy rates, the highest number of abortions in the world, the highest number of children raised in single-parent families, the highest rates of violent crime in an industrialized country, the highest youth suicide rates, and the highest proportion of drug users.

Elder Lindsay added:

> If we continue on our present course, we will experience further escalation in the destruction of families; more depression, divorce, violence and crime; more suicides and other tragic outcomes in the lives of our youth. Where rich, abundant family life is a priority, our society moves forward and progress is assured. Where families fail, societies disintegrate.[7]

What more fitting way for Satan to win the battle for mankind than to ensure that the majority who come to this earth do so under conditions controlled or influenced by Satan himself. The efforts of Satan have been evident in the destruction of the family, but of equal concern are his efforts to discourage traditional marriage and change the basic family structure.

According to national statistics there are substantially fewer marriages today than a decade ago. In fact, the National Center for Health Statistics documented a decline of more than 44 percent, from 1960 to 2000, in the annual number of marriages per 1,000 unmarried women.

Further information is found in a study from Rutgers University, titled "The State of Our Unions." This research completed by the National Marriage Project, an organization that studies current trends of marriage in America, revealed:

> Key social indicators suggest a substantial weakening of the institution of marriage. Americans have become less likely to marry. When they do marry their marriages are less happy....As an institution, marriage has lost much of its legal, religious and social meaning and authority. It has dwindled to a "couples relationship," mainly designed for the sexual and emotional gratification of each adult.
>
> Moreover, some elites seem to believe that support for marriage is synonymous with far-right political or religious views, discrimination against single parents, and tolerance of domestic violence.[8]

One of Satan's newest and most effective efforts has been in the selected choice of individuals to raise children without a traditional marriage partner. Political agendas by various anti-family organizations, as well as new legislation, promote the unholy practice of same sex marriages, encouraging gay individuals to adopt or give birth within perverted family structures. What better way to discourage family growth than by dissolving the very basis of procreation!

Famous gay relationships, as well as the not-so-famous, have recently obtained notoriety in their successful efforts to have and raise children without having to comply with the traditional family structure. In addition to these problems, an article in *Time Magazine* entitled, "Will Woman Still Need Men?" discusses the soon to be common practice of having babies without having sex; stating that *"We're only a few in vitro developments away from gender independence.... Thanks to in vitro fertilization, we can have babies without having sex."*[9]

One of the most disturbing events to undermine the sanctity of the family, and a possible prelude to other legislation around the world, is the passage of a bill by the Dutch government establishing full equal rights for gay couples, including full adoption rights. According to news reports, *"Lawmakers thumped their desks in approval when the vote passed 107-33,...scores of witnesses in the packed public gallery applauded and embraced."*[10] The bill received support from all three of the parliamentary factions in the government including the largest opposition party, the traditional Christian Democratic Alliance.

Our Church leaders, past and present, have spoken out against any relationship not in keeping with the sacred marriage covenant, as well as any unholy practice that would restrict family growth or terminate the lives of unborn children (see Proclamation to the World, Appendix C).

Joseph F. Smith, the sixth president of the Church, declared, *"God not only commends but he commands marriage."* He also offers this observation of the world's view on marriage in contrast to the Lord's plan:

> ...[*People*] are more and more being imbued with the selfish and ungodly idea that marriage is wrong and children a disgrace. The Church of Jesus Christ of Latter-day Saints takes an entirely opposite view, and believes in, and teaches as gospel truth, the first great scriptural commandment of God to man: "Be fruitful, and multiply and replenish the earth, and subdue it" (Genesis 1:28).[11]

The movement against marriage and family, first noted by early Church leaders, has now come to the forefront as a highly debated issue. Many prominent people have taken a stand against this change and its ensuing effects. In a recent book on parenthood in America, Dr. Laura Schlessinger expresses her concern:

> I often despair for the future. Families are fast becoming whatever anyone *says* a family is. The concept of family as a sacred vessel, strengthened by a committed, covenantal relationship between a man and a woman, for the safe passage of moral, generous, and loving children, is no longer venerated or even aspired to. It is, instead, mocked and denigrated as old-fashioned, patriarchal, and exclusive. At worst, it is ridiculed as an emblem of religious bigotry and intolerance.[12]

Satan will use any and all means to further his cause, from the power of the media to corrupt leaders who exert their values and influence upon nations. He has promised to buy and control armies, and reign with blood and terror. All this and more have we seen throughout history and will continue to see in the future. Speaking of Satan and his destructive methods, Gordon B. Hinckley stated:

> That war, so bitter, so intense, has gone on, and it has never ceased. It is the war between truth and error, between agency and compulsion, between the followers of Christ and those who have denied Him. His enemies have used every stratagem in that conflict. They've indulged in lying and deceit. They've employed money and wealth. They've tricked the minds of men. They've murdered and destroyed and engaged in every other unholy and impure practice to thwart the work of Christ.[13]

Not only has Lucifer brought about destruction by every means possible, but through his widespread influence great sums of money have been funneled into the promotion of family destruction. These contributions have come from countless individuals as well as a myriad of diverse corporations and government agencies. In 1999, Planned Parenthood received $176.5 million in government grants.[14] With the vast resources obtained from these benefactors, organizations promoting anti-family values and perverted interests continue to flourish.

One such organization, an international coalition campaigning to "save the earth," states their purpose is to create awareness and action on social issues, locally, nationally and globally. According to their mission statement they have impacted millions of people around the world. They declare the following as part of their global advertising campaign:

> Although one of the success stories of recent years has been the reduction of birth rates, the single greatest threat to our environment, to our resources, to our quality of life, may be too many people.... Ironically, too much life threatens life itself...Just as survival of the species historically depended on procreation, survival of the species now depends on restraining this impulse. The future of our children will depend on limiting the quantity and focusing on the quality of their lives. The worst predictions of 30 years ago have been averted by action. Conversely, apathy can nullify current predictions of future stability and lead to chaos.[15]

As the master of deceptive marketing, Satan will advance his cause in all mediums, in all countries, and with anyone who will open their minds to the smallest prompting. The mistaken belief that there will be a greater global benefit by raising only one child, or better still, "no children", is shared by many misguided individuals throughout the world and in our own country.

Even within the walls of Zion these opinions are expressed, as recently heard on a local public radio station in Salt Lake City. Under the guise of "saving our planet," this alarming editorial, although not the view of the radio station, was expressed by an outspoken listener: *"We seem to celebrate families of 9, 12, or even 17 children by one woman. The direct cost of supporting and sustaining this number of children by parents is miniscule compared to the price the earth must ultimately pay."*[16] This outcry to initiate more responsible care for the planet by having fewer children is based on unsubstantiated facts and information, a belief grounded in fear and ignorance.

Can we really believe the Lord in all his wisdom and glory would not provide sufficient resources for all his children? The answer is clear as we read in Doctrine and Covenants 104:17: *"For the earth is full, and there is enough and to spare; yea, I prepared all things, and have given unto the children of men to be agents unto themselves."* We are not living without sufficient resources, nor will we ever be. It is only a lack of human kindness, growing greed, and selfishness of those influenced by Satan, that cause many in the world to go without food, clothing, and the basic necessities of life. From the pages of Bruce R. McConkie's book, *Mormon Doctrine*, comes this authoritative statement:

> Today the cry is heard in some quarters that these statements calling upon parents to provide bodies for the spirit hosts of heaven are outmoded. Massive birth control programs are being sponsored on a national and international scale. Fears are expressed that the earth

cannot support the number of people that unrestricted births will bring. But God's decree and the counsel of the prophets remain unchanged.

> The real need is not to limit the number of earth's inhabitants, but to learn how to care for the increasing hosts which the Lord designs should inhabit this globe before the last allocated spirit has been sent here to gain a mortal body. Amid all the cries and pressure of the world, the position of the true Church remains fixed. God has commanded his children to multiply and fill the earth, and the earth is far from full.[17]

There are millions around the world who oppose the concept of zero population growth and many more who take a religious stand against birth control. Despite their efforts to stand up for right and wage the battle against Satan's onslaught, they may be loosing ground. An article published in *The New York Times* addressing the issue of over population in Europe, stated: *"There is no longer a single country in Europe where people are having enough children to replace themselves when they die."*[18] The picture worsens as we look at the figures from the World Population Reference Bureau. From 1997 to the year 2000 the population in Russia alone decreased by 2 million people. Worldwide there are now over 50 countries unable to replace their aging population due to the dramatic reduction in birth rate.

In the United States the birth rate has also declined. According to the US Census Bureau, there were 23.7 births in 1960 for each 1,000 people. Current estimates indicate only 14.2 for the year 2001. Further statistics provided by American Demographics confirm this trend, showing that married couples without children under 18 have steadily increased from 28.6 million households in 1995, to a projected 36.9 million in the year 2010.

Again, we only have to look at the cause to understand the effect. Although abortion was illegal in almost every country until the last half of the past century, by the late 1980's most countries had revised their laws. Currently 41 percent of the 193 countries in the world permit abortion without any restrictions. Even in the developed countries of Europe, no less than 28 of the 43 countries have legalized "abortion on demand."[19] The global success of Satan's efforts seems unstoppable; since 1973 abortions worldwide have reached over 1.3 billion.[20]

Even more shocking is the 1980 mandate by the government of China allowing couples only one child. In an effort to control population growth, 92 percent of the population in China must now comply with the "one-couple, one-child policy," as well as require couples to participate in birth control, sterilization, or forced abortions for all unauthorized pregnancies.[21] Because of the severe financial penalties couples face for not complying with this policy, much of the population has taken steps to curtail their own family growth by abandonment and death, resulting in "female infanticide."

A comprehensive study by two prominent researchers, G. William Skinner and Yuan Jianhua, has concluded that population control policies in China have resulted in families terminating the lives of over 808,000 newly born baby girls in one region of the country alone, drowning being the most common form of death.[22] In the year 2000, the government of China expressed their satisfaction in the "one-couple, one-child policy," stating that they had prevented at least 250 million births since 1980.[23] Offering further support of this policy, an editorial in the Communist Party newspaper, *The People's Daily*, asserted: "*We cannot just be content with the current success, we must* *make population control a permanent policy."*²⁴ With the introduction of ultrasound technology to China, sex determination can now be made in advance of birth, allowing China to become one of world leaders in surgical abortions with over 10 million performed each year.

However, China is not alone. Other countries such as Cuba, Romania, and Vietnam have reported very high abortion rates, while Afghanistan, Bangladesh, and India have similarly led the way in infant death. According to recent reports an estimated 6.7 million abortions take place in India every year.²⁵ This crime against humanity and offense to God does not end here. The *London Times* reports: *"More than 16 million baby girls in India are killed by their mothers or village midwives annually."*²⁶ Some babies are buried alive, interred in pots to suffocate, or have their mouths stuffed with wet clothes. Others are poisoned or slammed against walls.

Speaking about the great destruction of human life, President Wilford Woodruff shared these sobering thoughts:

> For there was a power that dwelt upon the earth in the form of thousands and millions of fallen spirits, one-third of the hosts of heaven, which had been cast out of heaven with the devil in the great rebellion, who remain in that condition and who do not possess tabernacles, and they make war upon the Saints of God, wherever or whenever they are found upon the earth, and upon all men; they seek to destroy the whole human family, and have done so from the beginning until the present day, and they have not ceased their labors, nor do they intend to while Satan remains unbound.²⁷

Here in America, the land preserved and blessed to bring forth the gospel, the battle between good and evil is at its most crucial juncture.

The lines are drawn, the boundaries set, and those who stand against the Lord's plan have spoken. *"The most merciful thing a large family can do for one of its infant members is to kill it,"*[28] stated Margaret Sanger, founder of Planned Parenthood. Her organization, which continues today, destroys hundreds of thousands of unborn children each year. Unfortunately, this is only one of many such organizations throughout the United States. As we look at the goals of these individuals and groups, is there any question whose side they stand on?

More than 421 million unborn babies have been killed chemically or surgically in the United States since the Supreme Court's decision legalized abortion in 1973.[29] From this well-known court case (Rowe vs. Wade), came a moral change in America. Although there are special circumstances justifying abortion, the law now allows a woman to obtain an abortion at any time and for any reason during her nine-month pregnancy. Not only does abortion come in direct conflict with the command to "multiply and replenish the earth," but it remains a form of murder, perpetuated by the adversary to destroy human life. Worse still, are the degenerating values it allows to develop within our own society. This statement from the Ohio Right to Life Society gives us much to think about: *"Abortion-on-demand is also corrupting the culture at-large by advancing the false idea that human beings can solve their problems or escape their pain through violence, killing, and abandonment."*[30]

At the present time there are over 16 million abortions performed in America each year.[31] With the recent approval of the RUD438 abortion pill, a drug designed for the convenience of those seeking an abortion, the termination of human life will certainly exceed current levels. Of further concern is the hope of many advocates, that in the hands of primary care providers, the drug will "mainstream" abortion in our society.

As we have seen, Satan by various means has succeeded in stopping billions of spirit children from obtaining bodies here upon the earth. This he does to thwart the Lord's plan. The pioneers who practiced plural marriage understood this and realized that their efforts would provide an opportunity for many spirit children to be born. Their large families were representative of their obedience to the Lord's commandment to "multiply and replenish the earth." One plural wife, Nancy Tracy, had these thoughts to share:

> How much more honorable it is for a man to marry two or three wives, support and care for them, nourish and cherish them, raise up lawful children, feed and clothe and educate them and prepare them for usefulness in life. I say how far superior to the sin and corruption of those who seek to destroy the life of the infant before it is born and after because their deeds have been evil.
>
> ...this work of the gathering and preparing for the second advent of the Messiah was spoken of by the ancient prophets...with an understanding heart we can know that this great event is near at hand by the signs of the times. And there has got to be a great work done and the people prepared to meet him and a holy place for him to come to.[32]

We all stand at the crossroads ready to embrace the future of mankind, a future that will be determined by our choice of good or evil. There is a course to follow, a decision we must make. Martin Luther King, one of the great advocates for truth and justice said, "*...there comes a time where one must take a position that is neither safe, nor* *politic, nor popular, but because—conscience tells one it is right."*[33] We must choose the right and move forward with courage, dedication and a desire to strengthen the family. Let us walk in the footsteps of the early Saints and accept the responsibility given to us to provide earthly tabernacles for waiting spirit children. And as we consider the future, let us prepare ourselves and our families and join with the Lord in His desire for us to bring forth a righteous posterity—children of *more than one.*

Daughters of Robert & Josepha Roberts. Used by permission of David Zolman

Chapter Eight

SAVING THE FAMILY

"...Even a small share in the affection, care and attention of a good husband would be far better than no husband or family at all."[1]
~ Helen Mar Whitney

The practice of plural marriage by church members in the 1800's was anchored in strong family values and achieved numerous objectives. One of the most important objectives was saving the family from the destructive influences that undermined the solidarity of the home. Not only was this an important goal for the early members of the Church, but also continues today as one of the most impassioned efforts of the Church of Jesus Christ of Latter-day Saints. It is a well-known fact that the health and strength of any nation is in direct proportion to the strength of the family. It was then, and still is today, the responsibility of every citizen to establish the laws and principles that strengthen the family and in so doing, strengthen the country. The early Saints took this responsibility to heart. They were able to achieve the goal of building strong and secure families by first taking steps to prevent the increase of divorce, infidelity and prostitution throughout their territory, as well as many other vices that plagued society.

Secondly, they provided the opportunity for many of Heavenly Father's children to be born and raised in loving homes, enjoying the blessings and benefits of a father, mother, brothers and sisters. These privileges were not reserved for a select few. Widows, single mothers, and orphans were all provided for and given the blessings of family life. One of the most effective ways these goals were accomplished was through the practice of plural marriage. By adhering to the objectives the Lord had in establishing plural marriage, they brought life not only to the barren desert but also to the Church as a whole.

> The principle [*plural marriage*] was explained to me in this way. There are two particular objects the Lord had in mind with many others—the one is to bring about the more perfect way of living—the human family having been degenerating for many generations, and the Lord has designed to give laws that will establish a system to bring about that which has been lost, and that will be done by men and woman governing their passions and feelings and live in every way according to the principles of charity and cleanliness, and to bring forth children that would be better developed in every way.
>
> Another grand object is this—there are millions of noble spirits in the spirit world who are anxiously waiting to take the bodies through channels that are pure and uncontaminated, and the more such bodies prepared, the greater rejoicing there is in the spirit world. There were other pure principles that were taught me by the apostles of the church and said it was one of the most sacred principles that had ever been revealed from heaven and could not be trifled with in the least, without bringing displeasure of the Lord upon men.[2]
>
> *~ Samuel Claridge*

It was their strong desire to fulfill this purpose that motivated early church members to step forward and accept the divine calling of plural marriage. Although our goals and objectives are similar today, would we have the same courage to make plural marriage part of our lives? Such a change in our culture and practices would not be easy. It would require an awareness, understanding and acceptance of the basic principles of marriage as found in the Old Testament and in the gospel teachings of Jesus Christ. It would also require certain changes in the laws of the land, in our social responsibility, and in the religious principles that make up the foundation of our society. This being accomplished, the Lord could then voice his approval through the latter-day prophet giving him permission to once again commence the practice of plural marriage in the Church. Then would a call go out to worthy members of the Church to bring about a fulfillment of this particular principle as established by the Lord.

It would be an extremely difficult challenge for most husbands and wives to accept the call. The very thought that plural marriage would be brought back under any circumstances, runs in direct conflict to the mindset of most Latter-day Saints as well as a majority of other Christian churches. Still, there are some people who, putting their prejudices aside, see an acute need for this divine plan to be restored. As they look at the desperate condition of mothers and children who have lost their husbands and fathers to sickness, wars, and tragedy, they see the urgent need to provide them with their physical needs in a stable environment. The material resources provided to destitute areas of the world by various humanitarian organizations, including the Mormon Church, are limited and in many circumstances, never reach those that are most in need. These are temporary solutions to a long-term problem. Could the restoration of plural marriage help resolve some of these difficulties?

Concerns have also been expressed regarding the declining birth rate throughout many parts of the world, particularly in those countries ravaged by war. Eligible males have decreased in great numbers, and many of those left are socially dysfunctional due to a life of alcoholism, drugs and unemployment. In these countries live many single sisters who are members of the Church of Jesus Christ of Latter-day Saints. Many have little or no hope for the future, no opportunity to marry a worthy priesthood holder, and no opportunity to establish a family conceived within the covenants of temple marriage. In those areas of the world members of the Church are few, and their prospects for eternal marriage—even fewer.

In addition to this worldwide problem, there are many in the Church concerned about the problem closer to home. In our own country there exists a silent force of single sisters—thousands who have been passed by in society's perception of the beautiful, popular or elite. These faithful sisters, as many in other countries, stand ready to share their lives with a worthy husband, fulfill their role of motherhood, and enjoy the blessings of family life. Whether a member living here or abroad, each sister should have the opportunity to fulfill the measure of her creation. As Sister Eliza R. Snow expressed so well during the early days of the Church: *"There is no sister so isolated, and her sphere so narrow but what she can do a great deal towards establishing the kingdom of God upon the earth."*[3]

It was the common belief of the sisters practicing plural marriage that *"establishing the kingdom of God upon the earth"* could best be accomplished through the divine role of motherhood, within the bonds of holy matrimony, and secured by the blessing of eternal increase.

Many of the sisters were outspoken in these basic beliefs and asserted their right to live, marry, and bear children as they saw fit. Helen Mar Whitney, with the insight and wisdom of a woman deep in the practice of plural marriage, asserted her view of the divine right of each and every woman:

…Let every woman have a husband and a home; and let every man have as many women as he can love, and as can love him, and as he is able to support, until all the women are provided for:…As the word of God has declared marriage to be honorable in all, so we must infer that His laws have made provision for the honorable marriage of all, and that every person of each sex is equally entitled to its rights and benefits.

…If love be refining and ennobling, if it be the spontaneous, instinctive birthright of all, and if our Creator has restricted its indulgence to the marriage relation, then marriage must be the right of all, or else God is not a benevolent being. But all nature and all revelation have demonstrated that He is a benevolent being, and it is both impious and absurd to believe that His laws have made no adequate provision for everyone to be married who wishes to be.…

The fault is not in nature nor in the laws of God but it is in the tyrannical laws and fashions of the artificial system of social life which now obtains among us. This system must be at fault, for it does not and cannot provide for the marriage of all; and many who desire to marry are forever deprived of husbands and homes; while the

Photo used by permission, Utah State Historical Society, all rights reserved.

system of polygamy does provide for all, and is, therefore, the only system which is in harmony with divine and natural law....[4]

Although the rights of women today have been expanded and protected, not all women have the right to a husband, home and family simply by the fact that they are women. The practice of plural marriage is still forbidden by the laws of the land. Since God has declared that marriage is for all and that he loves His children equally, then we must assume that certain changes will be inevitable. Our acceptance of these changes in the future is dependent on our appreciation of the past. This appreciation can be acquired by understanding how the principle of plural marriage would affect us in our own lives. This may be accomplished by creating a simulation of the principle in our day—how would it start, how would it be organized and who would accept the call.

Reinstating the principle of plural marriage in the Church today would first require a divine mandate issued through the prophet to the membership of the Church. This would be in conjunction with necessary changes in the laws of the land. Then certain organizational steps would need to be initiated. Bishops and stake presidents would more than likely receive guidelines established by a special department set up within the Church to determine the qualifications of potential participants. These might include worthiness, health issues, accommodations and financial ability, to name a few. After these items had been considered, the appropriate papers would be submitted to a board of review. As part of the process to determine who would participate, the board would probably follow much the same procedure as for new missionaries—recommending worthy couples to the First Presidency, who would subsequently extend a formal call "to serve."

We can assume the second step in the process would involve single sisters over the age of 21, as well as divorced and single mothers, being contacted and interviewed to establish their interest in participating in the "program". A database containing a profile of each couple and each sister could then be established. As the call was extended to participating couples, so would the invitation be given to sisters who had established their eligibility and worthiness. Much like the sisters in the early days of the Church, each would have their free agency to choose whom they would marry. To expedite this process in our day, each sister would no doubt receive a composite of families from which she could choose, allowing her the agency to select an eternal companion and family. At the same time, the couple who had been chosen would have the opportunity to accept the proposal and welcome the sister or sisters into their family.

Although the program could be expanded to encompass the Church worldwide, the initial program would more than likely be limited to North America where economic and political stability exists, as well as the legal right to have any number of children. Sisters throughout the world unable to enjoy the blessings of an eternal marriage in their own land, would be given the opportunity to come to the "Land of Promise." Here they would be able to enter into in a marriage with a worthy priesthood holder, with the possibility of gaining exaltation and eternal increase.

Our present society is much more complex, and issues exist today that were not prevalent in early pioneer days. For this reason, a very different organizational structure would need to be established in order to actually enact the practice of plural marriage. There would need to be sufficient resources to oversee the success of the program, in particular, an ongoing system to insure that all families participating in the program are conforming to the laws of the land as well as the strict church guidelines. Monthly contact by Church officials with the sisters in each family would help to insure that all needs are being met, in addition to offering support as they are integrated into the family structure.

It is obvious that the early Saints experienced many advantages in plural marriage compared to monogamous marriages. As we consider how life in the principle would be in our own lives, we can see that there would be similar benefits. For example, one would be the added support of sister-wives in the home when a mother is absent or unable to perform her duties. Sister-wives could quickly compensate for any situation such as sickness, work, or other responsibilities that may inhibit the normal function of the family. In addition, each wife would have the opportunity to reach her full potential in the areas of education, service, career or other special interests, as well as being a successful wife and mother in the home without sacrificing the needs of others. This would allow the family to always have a loving mother available for the children and a supportive wife to sustain the husband.

Emmeline Wells (front center) and other sister-wives

As a strong advocate of plural marriage, Emmeline Wells expressed similar views:

Photo used by permission, Utah State Historical Society, all rights reserved.

The world says polygamy makes women inferior to men—we think differently. Polygamy gives women more time for thought, for mental culture, more freedom of action, a broader field of labor, inculcates liberality and generosity, develops more fully the spiritual elements of life, fosters purity of thought and gives wider scope to benevolence....and leads women more directly to God, the fountain of all truth.[5]

As it was in the past, so would it be today. Love, companionship, and support of the husband would be multiplied, as would be the case for each individual in the home. In consideration of the old adage "behind every good man is a good woman," the husband would find an unending reserve of support, strength, counsel, wisdom and experience within his own family. Writing in his journal, Charles O. Card, founder of Cardston, Alberta, Canada, expressed his joy in the spiritual benefits of having more than one wife: *"When a man has a quorum of wives that pray as faithfully for my safety, he is much inspired by faith for deliverance and feels always to bless them. God Bless the faithful wives..."*[6]

Other blessings and benefits would be realized from this program as the needs of more and more were being met. Single sisters would be brought out of obscurity to enjoy the blessings of marriage and family life, giving them the opportunity to fulfill the Lord's commandment to multiply and replenish the earth. Single and divorced mothers would find happiness and security in being married to a worthy priesthood holder, and children who have lived without a complete family would now have a loving father in the home. Although there are many couples who would choose to reject this responsibility, there are others who would welcome the call—giving their time, talents, and resources to bless the lives of others, while "saving the family" and helping to build up the Lord's kingdom here upon the earth.

There were many Latter-day Saints in the past that accepted this call. Having gained a testimony of its divine nature, they struggled through many trials and difficulties to leave us a great heritage and promise. One such sister, Nancy Tracy a plural wife, speaks of her husband and shares her testimony of plural marriage:

> During all this journey, my 14-year-old son had to take the charge of everything. We got home in Ogden City on the 4th day of July and my husband died on the 25th of August following, 1858. He now sleeps in the Ogden Cemetery. He was an honest, upright man and died in full faith of all the principles of our most holy religion and was a firm believer in the celestial or plural order of marriage which had been revealed from God to Joseph Smith as a pure and holy principle. But to many it comes so in contrast with tradition and the views and opinion of the pious in this age of the world that it is thought to be an unpardonable sin for a man to have more than one wife. But when God speaks and commands, who shall we obey, him or man? I prefer the former.
>
> I have lived in this order of plural marriage, have had one daughter born in polygamy that is now an honorable wife and mother, and it is a pure principle and saving in its nature, and all that are conversant with the Bible must know that the ancient patriarchs and prophets had more wives than one, but God is the same. If he revoked

Photo used by permission, Utah State Historical Society, all rights reserved.

this command because of the wickedness of the people, it is no sign but what he can command again.⁷

We may never fully understand the pains the early pioneers endured in establishing the principle of plural marriage, but we can see the results of their efforts in our culture, posterity, and in the leadership that now stands as a witness of Jesus Christ. It is this great leadership that extends the challenge to bring the blessings of the gospel to each and every person. In a recent general conference President Gordon B. Hinckley expressed:

> My brethren and sisters, I would hope, I would pray, that each of us, having participated in this great conference, would resolve to seek those who need help, who are in desperate and difficult circumstances and lift them in the spirit of love into the embrace of the Church, where strong hands and loving hearts will warm them, comfort them, sustain them, and put them on the way of happy and productive lives.⁸

In following the counsel of the prophet, could we consider plural marriage as a vehicle to provide *"strong hands and loving hearts"* to the widows, divorced mothers and single sisters? We have the ability, resources, and the knowledge to effectively bring the blessings of the gospel to everyone here upon the earth. Each person can do his or her part in meeting this challenge by gaining an understanding and appreciation of plural marriage as established by the Lord.

Every parent who has shared in their daughter's disappointment of life without marriage and children, can appreciate the need to pray that someday this great principle will be restored. We all know of a special sister who struggles to be both father and mother in the home, who earnestly seeks a worthy role model for her children as well as the companionship of a husband.

They, too, need our prayers. And for the many thousands of sisters around the world who have no promise of eternal marriage in this life, let us open the door to the joys and blessings that so many of us partake of. Let us all reach out—every father, mother, friend and brother—to those in need. Let us all pray for *more than one*.

Chapter Nine

RESTORING ALL THINGS

"...Whatever God requires is right, no matter what it is, although we may not see the reason thereof till long after the events transpire."[1]
~ *Joseph Smith*

As we review the Old Testament, there is no question that the practice of plural marriage was approved by God during Biblical times and practiced by many of the great prophets as well. Abraham, Isaac and Jacob, to mention a few, had numerous wives in addition to many concubines, who were wives of a lesser status. As indicated in D&C 132:37, the Lord not only commanded these prophets and others to practice plural marriage, but He did so from the beginning of creation. The scripture goes on to state that the Lord gave them eternal exaltation because of their obedience to the principle, a clear indication that plural marriage was acceptable to the Lord.

Some scholars have supposed that even Christ himself practiced plural marriage. Apostle Orson Hyde expressed this thought as early as 1855 in his address to the Saints in the Salt Lake Tabernacle: "...*Mary, Martha, and others were his wives.*"[2] Although an unpopular doctrine in the 1800's, it gained much greater acceptance in the past century by New Testament scholars.

Plural marriage was not only a way of life mentioned throughout the scriptures, but in many cases it has been a directive from God. These directives, as well as the organization of His Church, would be continued in the latter days. Thus, there is an understandable association between the principle of plural marriage and the restoration of the gospel. To better understand this association, we must gain an insight as to how the various dispensations relate to these, the last days.

There have been many "dispensations" since the creation of the world—designated periods of time when at least one person on the earth, holding the keys of the priesthood, has been authorized to dispense the gospel to all mankind. Each dispensation has been unique in its authority and purpose; for example, the dispensation of Adam represented the start of mankind, and Noah's dispensation represented the flood. Abraham, Moses, and Jesus Christ each had their specific authority and purpose, which associated them with a dispensation, as did many others in the Bible and Book of Mormon.

The principle of plural marriage, along with all other "principles, powers and blessings," was a part of each specific dispensation. They have all been combined into what is now the final dispensation, the restoration of all things as described in Acts 3:20-21: *"And he shall send Jesus Christ, which before was preached unto you: Whom the heaven must receive until the times of restitution of all things, which God hath spoken by the mouth of all his holy prophets since the world began."*

This "restitution of all things" is the period of time starting with the restoration of the gospel to Joseph Smith. It is referred to as the sum total of all dispensations, or the "dispensation of the fullness of times." President John Taylor further clarified:

We have had in different ages various dispensations;...But in the dispensation of the fullness of times a combination or a fullness, a completeness of all those dispensations was to be introduced among the human family....If there was anything associated with the Melchizedek Priesthood in all its forms, powers, privileges and blessings at any time or in any part of the earth, it would be restored in the last  days. If there was anything connected with the Aaronic Priesthood, that also would be developed in the last times.

If there was anything associated with the Apostleship and Presidency that existed in the days of Jesus, or that existed on this continent, it would be developed in the last times. For this is the dispensation of the fullness of times, embracing all other times, <u>all principles</u>, all powers, all manifestations, all Priesthoods and the powers thereof that have existed in any age, in any part of the world. For, "Those things which never have been revealed from the foundation of the world, but have been kept hid from the wise and prudent, shall be revealed unto babes and sucklings in this the dispensation of the fullness of times."[3]

As we consider the fact that "all principles" will be restored in this dispensation, logically, the principle of plural marriage will be included. Writing about plural marriage and the restoration, Apostle Mark E. Petersen, expressed the importance of Joseph Smith and his acceptance of the principle. He affirmed the following: *"The Prophet Joseph did not wish to enter polygamy. It was farthest from his mind.*

<small>Photo used by permission, Utah State Historical Society, all rights reserved.</small>

But he was the restorer, and through him 'all things' must be restored. Hence under the persuasion of the Lord, he accepted it."[4]

Although it was brought forth during the time of Joseph Smith and withdrawn from the Church a short time later, it still must be brought back to its full measure and re-established, as defined by the word "restore," which is according to Webster, *"to put or bring back into existence or use"* and *"to bring back to or put back into a former or original state."*[5] In either case the use of the word "restore" by President Taylor and others is very clear.

The Prophet Joseph Smith speaking of the Lord's return, supported this reasoning in the following statement: *"Now the purpose in Himself in the winding up scene of the last dispensation is that all things pertaining to that dispensation should be conducted precisely in accordance with the preceding dispensations."*[6] How then, can all things be "conducted precisely" without the principle of plural marriage being practiced again by the members of the Church? Obviously, plural marriage is a significant part of the restoration and will be re-instituted among the saints at some future time.

Others have expressed this understanding as well. Wilford Woodruff, the fourth president of the Church of Jesus Christ of Latter-day Saints, concluded:

> The reason why the Church and Kingdom of God cannot advance without the Patriarchal Order of Marriage [*plural marriage*] is that it belongs to this dispensation just as baptism for the dead does, or any law or ordinance that belongs to a dispensation. Without it the Church cannot progress.[7]

Even though the Church cannot progress without all things being restored in this dispensation, there may be another aspect of President Woodruff's comments yet to consider. Perhaps his statement reflects a belief that the Church could not progress in its goal to bring the gospel to the entire world.

The Lord requires that His gospel be preached to the entire world before His return, as stated in Doctrine & Covenants 58:64-65:

> For, verily, the sound must go forth from this place into all the world, and unto the uttermost parts of the earth—the gospel must be preached unto every creature, with signs following them that believe. And behold the Son of Man cometh. Amen.

If the gospel is to be brought to the world, then the world must have access to the Church. It is a well-known fact that the Church of Jesus Christ of Latter-day Saints is one of the fastest growing Christian churches in the world. According to *U.S. News & World Report* magazine, the Church is growing at an extraordinary rate, stating: *"If current trends hold, experts say Latter-day Saints could number 265 million worldwide by 2080, second only to Roman Catholics among Christian bodies."*[8] Still we must address the issue that not all the world has access to membership in the Church.

To accomplish this task, walls must come down, borders opened and "all people and cultures" must be accepted into the Church. As an official representative of the Lord, the Apostle Bruce R. McConkie addressed members during a general conference of the Church and gave the following prophecy:

> Looking ahead, we see the gospel preached in all nations and to every people with success attending. We see the Lord break down the barriers so that the world of Islam and the world of Communism can hear the message of the restoration;...
>
> We see congregations of the covenant people worshipping the Lord in Moscow and Peking and Saigon. We see Saints of the Most High raising their voices in Egypt and India and Africa. We see stakes of Zion in all parts of the earth; and Israel, the chosen people, gathering into these cities of holiness, as it were, to await the coming of their King.[9]

We have seen many of these things come to pass. Unfortunately, not "*...every nation, and kindred, and tongue and people*" as commanded in Doctrine & Covenants 133:37, will be able to receive the blessings of the gospel. To do so would require many to relinquish the very customs, traditions and lifestyles (plural marriage), that have established them as a unique people in the world—in particular, the numerous groups of Asians and Africans who practice this form of marriage, as well as those in the Jewish and Islamic cultures.

The Church desires to bring everyone into the fold, however current Church policy prohibits certain groups of people in various countries around the world, who practice plural marriage as part of their culture, from being baptized into the Church. President Gordon B. Hinckley in his address to the membership of the Church during General Conference in November of 1998, declared: "*Even in countries where civil or religious law allows polygamy, the Church teaches that marriage must be monogamous and does not accept into its membership those practicing plural marriage.*"[10]

According to the recent studies done by Altman and Ginat in their book, *Polygamous Families in Contemporary Society*, it was determined that out of the hundreds of cultures throughout the world, 78% practice some form of plural marriage. They went on to state: *"Thus polygyny* (a man with more than one wife), *appears to be common practice among world cultures."*[11]

There are millions of individuals throughout the world practicing plural marriage that may soon be taught by the Lord's army of missionaries. When they receive a testimony of the restored gospel and desire membership in the Lord's Church, will husbands be asked to cast off their plural wives and children? Will other cultures throughout the world be asked to change their lifestyle to meet the laws and moral requirements set down by this country? This does not address the many thousands in our own country who practice plural marriage, including the estimated 50,000 in the western states alone. If the laws of the land change, will these people be asked to choose only one wife in order to have membership in the Lord's Church, or will the Lord in His eternal struggle to preserve the family, again give His permission to live this divine principle?

This has been a concern for Church leaders since the time of Joseph Smith. In the Prophet's speech to the Saints in Nauvoo, he addressed the issue of plural marriage and the effect the Church would have on other cultures, in particular those who would eventually accept the gospel of Jesus Christ. Joseph did this to not only test the waters to see how members would feel about this new doctrine, but *"…to throw out something for the people to reflect upon…,"*[12] knowing that soon they would be called upon to live this celestial law. From his personal journal, Joseph Lee Robinson relates the following story regarding his visit to the Nauvoo meeting and the Prophet's comments:

And again while speaking to the people in that place [*a grove near the temple*] he [*Joseph Smith*] supposed a case. He said, "Suppose we send one of our Elders to Turkey or India or to a people where it was lawful to have several wives, where they practiced polygamy and he should say to them, 'Your laws are not good, you should put away your plural wives;' what would they do to him? They would kick them out of their realm," said he. "What right had he to speak against their laws and usages?" Said he, "God does not care what laws they make if they will live up to them."

The Prophet went on preaching the Gospel...as the Lord had revealed the principle of plural marriage to him. And had informed him that the time had fully come that that doctrine should be taught and practiced by his people, the Latter-day Saints, as it was a very important item pertaining to the fullness of the Gospel. He deemed it wisdom to throw out something for the people to reflect upon, that they might begin to digest that very important doctrine, which belongs to the dispensation of the fullness of times. But prior to this he had besought the Lord to take this injunction from him, that he might not have the responsibility of introducing and putting in practice that order of things, because of the great opposition it would meet and because of the traditions of the people, but it came to pass the Lord instead of releasing him from that burden, He sent an Holy Angel with a drawn sword unto him, saying unto him, "Joseph unless you go to and immediately teach that principle (plural marriage), and put the same in practice, that he (Joseph) should be slain...."

In the morning he declared the law in Zion should favor plural wives. It surprised me much as it was the first intimation that I had ever had, as we remarked, in favor of polygamy. I retired to my dinner. Several of the brethren stopped into my house and we talked about the preaching. I remarked to them that it was not likely that we should have the privilege of taking more wives, but that the law would be framed so that they that had several wives could retain them…

The meeting passed and the day also, and two or three days passed away and it was in my mind constantly. I felt satisfied that it was of God, for the Spirit bore that testimony to me. It came to pass that on Wednesday morning following as I was working with E. T. Benson, I received the first revelation upon that subject. It came as a flash of lightning to my mind. I stopped short, saying, "I have received a revelation, Brother Benson." "What is it?" said he. "I will tell you. Inasmuch as the Lord reveals the law, that shall give the brethren a right to bring his five wives and enjoy them in Zion, and inasmuch as you and I are members of the Church of Jesus Christ in full fellowship, it cannot prohibit us from having more than one wife." And said he, "That is true."

That was the first revelation that I received on polygamy and also the first that Brother Ezra T. Benson received, except what the Prophet said the Sabbath before. But it was not the last that I received, for it continued to be revealed to me from time to time. As the scriptures saith, the Lord giveth line upon line, precept upon precept, a little here and there a little, and so he leadeth his saints along from step to step.

But that one word from the Prophet gave me a starting point. It was as Alma in the Book of Mormon explained. The word implanted in my heart as a good seed sown in good ground. It was received in faith. It commenced to swell and it sprouted and grew from faith to a perfect knowledge so that I can say as Paul, if any man or angel from heaven shall preach any other Gospel than we have preached and ye have received, let him be accursed. So can I say with propriety, if any man or an angel from heaven comes and preaches any other doctrine than what the Prophet Joseph did preach, if he says that polygamy is not of God, I do verily know, he lies. Therefore, let him be accursed.

And now, my dear readers while I am on this subject I propose to make known unto you in my weak and clumsy way of writing, how the Lord revealed to me the truth of the doctrine of plural marriage or polygamy....

As we have remarked, I never had received one word from any man living except that one word from the Prophet, only as the Holy Ghost taught me. It also taught me some little of the future destiny of this people, as I remarked to some, being interrogated as to what would become of this people, this being soon after the martyrdom of Joseph and Hyrum.

The remarkable vision in which the Lord revealed to me, unworthy me, the certainty or the truth of that very remarkable, sacred and interesting doctrine. Pertaining to the fullness of the Gospel of the Son of God, which had to be revealed in the dispensation of the fullness of times, or at the commencement of that dispensation. As the Father had a large number of spirits, very intelligent, noble spirits, spirits that had been kept back in reserve to come forth to be born under or in the priesthood, to perform a certain very important work, this is what the Lord meant "When I will raise up seed unto me, I will command my people." The time now had fully arrived and it became necessary to command His people.[13]

For Latter-day Saints plural marriage is a fulfillment of prophecy, an essential part of the restoration; but to many others who are not yet members of the Church, this form of marriage is an unchangeable way of life—a way of life that unfortunately will keep millions of righteous people from enjoying the blessings of the gospel until this practice is brought back to the Church.

The gospel must be available to all of Heavenly Father's children in order to fulfill the prophecies of old. This was reaffirmed by Orson Pratt while speaking at a semi-annual conference of the Church: "*If God sees proper to accomplish this great work of restoration—the restitution of all things, it will include what the Prophet Moses has said, and it will bring back with it a plurality of wives.*"[14] With this in mind we must realize that the prophecies of old have been and will continue to be fulfilled.

The Prophet Isaiah foretold the return of plural marriage in the last days, stating in verse one of the fourth chapter of Isaiah: "*And in that day seven women shall take hold of one man, saying, We will eat our own bread, and wear our own apparel: only let us be called by thy name, to take away our reproach.*" It is important to understand the full meaning of this scripture and how it applies to each of us in these, the latter days. This scripture is one of the most significant messages concerning our participation in plural marriage.

As we examine the statement "*seven woman shall take hold of one man,*" we find this applies to the current state of affairs existing throughout the world. The Bible (Isaiah 3:25), defines this statement as a "*scarcity of men due to wars,*"[15] which is evident as we look at current statistics. According to the Carter Center, a human rights organization based in Atlanta, Georgia, there are currently between 30 to 40 ongoing wars around the world.

A further study by the Carnegie Commission on Preventing Deadly Conflict, concluded that since 1989, "*over 4 million people world wide have been killed in violent conflicts.*"[16] Further statistics show that one in every 200 people in the world today is a refugee or is displaced as a result of war. Other sources indicate that many of the countries involved in these wars are facing a dramatic change in the ratio of men to women due to the high mortality rate of males. This is a fulfillment of Isaiah's prophecy in part—a scarcity of men due to wars.

In the balance of the scripture we find the following words, *"We will eat our own bread, and wear our own apparel: only let us be called by thy name,..."* This refers to the determination and concern of women who will do all that they can to take care of themselves, but plea for the opportunity to be married. The last part of the scripture stating, *"to take away our reproach"* specifically refers to the blessing denied these sisters—the blessing to bear and raise children.

This reasoning is confirmed in Luke 1:24-25, which speaks of Elisabeth, the mother of John the Baptist, who was *"stricken in years,"* yet miraculously gave birth to a son as promised by an angel, taking away her reproach or "barrenness" as referenced in the Bible. The last part of Isaiah's prophecy is currently being fulfilled as we find the birth rate in many parts of the world declining because women are barren. Wives are without husbands, and single women are unable to find men to provide the security and stability needed for family life.

The re-establishment of plural marriage by the Lord will fulfill the balance of the prophecy by Isaiah, giving sisters in many countries the opportunity to be married, bear children and enjoy the blessings of a family. This understanding is confirmed in the words of President George Albert Smith. Speaking to the Saints on the institution of plural marriage, he concluded:

> It is true that the principle of plurality of wives was adopted by the Church of Latter-day Saints in consequence of the revelation and commandment which God gave Joseph Smith, and which, through

him, were laid upon the heads of this people; and we quote the passages that we do quote, in relation to the principle of celestial marriage from the Old and New Testament, to prove that God is consistent with himself; that if he revealed to his Saints in the last days, the doctrine of plurality of wives, it was in fulfillment of the prophecy of Isaiah and others of the Prophets, and in accordance with the example which was set by Abraham, Jacob, Moses, and by holy men of ancient days.[17]

As we consider the prophecy of Isaiah, let us also consider the words of another great author, *"It was the best of times, it was the worst of times...."*[18] Although written about another time and place far in our past, how applicable it is to our world today as we look at the many changes dramatically affecting our lives. We see the best of times as disease and hunger are declining, freedom and prosperity are enjoyed, and people around the world prepare for the coming of the Lord. On the other hand, we see the worst of times as Satan strengthens his grip on mankind. Hearts fail, wickedness increases and human kindness is abandoned. Depending upon our degree of faith, hope and spirituality, we will embrace either one perspective or the other. In either case the work of the Lord will go on, all things will be restored and the Lord will come. Despite the feeble efforts of man, God controls all things, as John Taylor explained:

> ...whatever the opinions and ideas of men may be, it will be found at last that the Lord rules, manipulates and manages the affairs of men, of nations and of the world, and therefore, neither this nation nor any other nation can do anything more than God permits. He sets up one nation, and puts down another, according to the counsels of

his own will. And he has done this from the beginning, whether men believe it or not.[19]

We have begun to witness His influence as it spreads over the nations of the world. He has sent many of the great and noble ones to help prepare mankind for the changes that need to take place before the Lord's Second Coming. Speaking of these prophetic changes, Elder Orson F. Whitney, an early apostle, makes this observation:

It tells me that Providence is over all, and that he holds the nations in the hollow of his hand; that he is using not only his covenant people, but other peoples as well, to consummate a work, stupendous, magnificent, and altogether too arduous for this little handful of Saints to accomplish by and of themselves....

Nor is he limited in the choice of instruments to his own people. He sways the scepter over all nations, and they are all playing into his hands, knowingly or unknowingly....good and great men, not bearing the Priesthood, but possessing profundity of thought, great wisdom, and a desire to uplift their fellows, have been sent by the Almighty into many nations, to give them, not the fullness of the Gospel, but that portion of truth that they were able to receive and wisely use.[20]

Through the Lord's divine power, we are witnessing the fulfillment of Isaiah's prophecy. This can be seen as millions throughout the world

Photo used by permission, Utah State Historical Society, all rights reserved.

and many thousands in our own country have accepted plural marriage not only as a way of life but as a divine principle and a way to strengthen and enlarge the family. Although not advocated by the Church of Jesus Christ of Latter-day Saints, there are many groups speaking out in favor of its advantages, supporting its Biblical beginnings, and promoting it through various forms of media. Many Christian churches and organizations have approved the practice of plural marriage, as well as political groups who are lobbying for changes in the laws of the land. These changes will help bring about the restoration of all things and enable this form of marriage to be morally accepted, legally binding and divinely approved. The spirit of plural marriage is indeed upon the land, and preparation has begun for a return—of *more than one*.

Chapter Ten

CONCLUSION

"...Every person who reads and reflects upon these statements, even if he has but little capacity for thinking, must admit that they contain a great amount of truth and common sense."[1]

~ Helen Mar Whitney

As we have seen and understood so many times, the Lord had His purposes in establishing the principle of plural marriage among the early saints. Unfortunately, because of the changes in the laws of the land and the conditions that were brought to bear upon the Church, President Wilford Woodruff, after receiving revelation on this matter issued the "Manifesto" in 1890. This document and the 1904 "Second Manifesto", eventually led to the termination of plural marriages within the Church. It later became a violation resulting in excommunication for those who participated in plural marriage as defined by the laws of the land.

Nevertheless, in the Church today there remains sufficient keys and authority to continue the practice of plural marriage. This authority is the power to administer the ordinance that would seal a man and woman for time and all eternity. The Prophet Elijah restored this authority in the Kirtland Temple as the power to bind on earth what shall be bound in heaven. This authority was passed down from Joseph Smith to the apostles and has remained in our church through succession to the present day. It is not a matter of authority that has halted plural marriage in the Church, but rather permission from the Lord. He has temporarily withdrawn this permission which is given only through the prophet of the Church. Although there lies within the Church the authority, keys and knowledge to re-establish plural marriage, doing so would require permission from the Lord, through his holy prophet, to once again practice this divine principle.

Aside from that mandate, there still remains within the Church a limited form of plural marriage. Those husbands who have lost a beloved spouse and are left alone in this world can still be married for time and eternity to another wife, provided they are sealed by one with authority. This covenant, which is not bound by the grave, allows for the continuation of relationships throughout the eternities. Likewise, our ancestors who had more than one wife in their lifetime may be sealed to each by proxy, thus permitting the continuation of their marriages.

It is clear that all marriages continued in heaven will involve participation in plural marriage. Whether instituted in this life or the next, it will be a part of our eternal existence. Many early church members understood this concept and accepted plural marriage as a great blessing in their life. Likewise, there were those that saw it as a great trial but came to realize that all trials are truly blessings. Whether a blessing or a trial, those that lived a life in the principle did so with the understanding that they were preparing the way for the establishment of the Lord's Kingdom. Speaking of their sacrifice, George Q. Cannon shares his thoughts of the past and hopes for the future:

No great principles, like those to which we are wedded, no great work like that in which we are engaged, can be established in the earth, in the present condition of mankind at least, without great sacrifice on the part of those connected with it. We need not expect anything else than this. The Lord through the Prophet Joseph Smith, in early church revelations, told to the Church: You are laying the foundation of a great work; how great you know not.

And the same words are just as applicable to us today, notwithstanding the growth of the work up to the present time. We with the light we now possess even, cannot conceive of its greatness. It has not entered into our hearts, neither are we capable of conceiving of it. But we our laying its foundation, nevertheless; and God has chosen us for this work. He has inspired us, and he has blessed us thus far in our endeavor to carry it out, and he will continue to do so to the end; and victory and glory will be the result of our faith and our diligence in keeping his commandments.[2]

Early members of the Church who participated in plural marriage laid the groundwork for the building up of the Lord's kingdom here upon the earth. During a time of great persecution, hardship and sacrifice, they rose up to establish a principle that would have an eternal effect on generations of church members, as well as the divine destiny of this country. From a conviction to follow the Lord's command to "multiply and replenish the earth," came individuals of remarkable strength and courage, those that have left an everlasting testimony of plural marriage. As a legacy to us, Eliza R. Snow left the following:

In Nauvoo I had the first intimation, or at least the first understanding, that the practice of a plurality of wives would be introduced into the Church. The thought was very repugnant to my feelings, and in direct opposition to my educational prepossessions; but when I reflected that this was the dispensation of the fullness of times, embracing all other dispensations, it was plain that plural marriage must be included; and I consoled myself with the idea that it was a long way in the distance, beyond the period of my mortal existence, and that, of course, I should not have it to meet. However, it was announced to me that the "set time" had come—that God had commanded his servants to establish the order, by taking additional wives.

It seemed for awhile as though all the traditions, prejudices, and superstitions of my ancestry, for many generations, accumulated before me in one immense mass; but God, who had kept silence for centuries, was speaking; I knew it, and had covenanted in the waters of baptism to live by every word of his, and my heart was still firmly set to do his bidding.

I was sealed to the prophet, Joseph Smith, for time and eternity, in accordance with the celestial law of marriage which God had revealed, the ceremony being performed by a servant of the Most High—authorized to officiate in sacred ordinances.

This, one of the most important events of my life, I have never had cause to regret. The more I comprehend the pure and ennobling principle of plural marriage, the more I appreciate it. It is a necessity in the salvation of the human family—a necessity in redeeming woman from the curse, and the world from its corruptions.

When I entered into it, my knowledge of what it was designed to accomplish was very limited; had I then understood what I now understand, I think I should have hailed its introduction with joy, in consideration of the great good to be accomplished. As it was, I received it because I knew that God required it.[3]

Whether it is a call given to the early saints or to us in this present day, it has been and will continue to be those that have the faith and obedience that will answer the call. As the Prophet Joseph Smith so profoundly stated, *"Whatever God requires is right, no matter what it is, although we may not see the reason thereof till long after the events transpire."*[4] With this in mind we need to consider the possibility that within the near future all things will be restored to their fullness in this, the last dispensation. This means that plural marriage will once again be a calling sent forth among the Latter-day Saints.

As we look back to the foundation the early saints provided, we should also look forward to the work that must go on in the future. In a talk entitled "Look to the Future," President Gordon B. Hinckley gave us this instruction:

> We cannot detract from their accomplishments. We cannot add to their glory. We can only look back with reverence, appreciation, respect, and resolution to build on what they have done. The time has now come to turn about and face the future. This is a season of a thousand opportunities. It is ours to grasp and move forward. What a wonderful time it is for each of us to do his or her small part in moving the work of the Lord on to its magnificent destiny.[5]

We must grasp the moment and help fulfill the promise of the future. The restoration of the gospel has come forth, signs have been

Illustration by Lester B. Lee, used by permission, all rights reserved.

given and soon there will be a great change upon the land. Soon we will encounter new and glorious opportunities to build upon the foundation that was provided by the early members of the Church. As reflected in the words of Joseph Smith, we must be spiritually primed, morally strengthened and ready to receive the call—a call for *more than one.*

> I have tried for a number of years to get the minds of the Saints prepared to receive the things of God; but we frequently see some of them, after suffering all they have for the work of God, will fly to pieces like glass as soon as anything comes that is contrary to their traditions: they cannot stand the fire at all. How many will be able to abide a celestial law, and go through and receive their exaltation, I am unable to say, as many are called, but few are chosen.[6]
>
> ~ *Joseph Smith*

Appendix A

Doctrine and Covenants Section 132

Revelation given through Joseph Smith the Prophet, at Nauvoo, Illinois, recorded on July 12, 1843, by William Clayton in the upstairs room of the brick store. This revelation relates to the new and everlasting covenant, including the eternity of the marriage covenant or plurality of wives.

1 Verily, thus saith the Lord unto you my servant Joseph, that inasmuch as you have inquired of my hand to know and understand wherein I, the Lord, justified my servants Abraham, Isaac, and Jacob, as also Moses, David and Solomon, my servants, as touching the principle and doctrine of their having many wives and concubines—

2 Behold, and lo, I am the Lord thy God, and will answer thee as touching this matter.

3 Therefore, prepare thy heart to receive and obey the instructions which I am about to give unto you; for all those who have this law revealed unto them must obey the same.

4 For behold, I reveal unto you a new and an everlasting covenant; and if ye abide not that covenant, then are ye damned; for no one can reject this covenant and be permitted to enter into my glory.

5 For all who will have a blessing at my hands shall abide the law which was appointed for that blessing, and the conditions thereof, as were instituted from before the foundation of the world.

6 And as pertaining to the new and everlasting covenant, it was instituted for the fulness of my glory; and he that receiveth a fulness thereof must and shall abide the law, or he shall be damned, saith the Lord God.

7 And verily I say unto you, that the conditions of this law are these: All covenants, contracts, bonds, obligations, oaths, vows, performances, connections, associations, or expectations, that are not made and entered into and sealed by the Holy Spirit of promise, of him who is anointed, both as well for time and for all eternity, and that too most holy, by revelation and commandment through the medium of mine anointed, whom I have appointed on the earth to hold this power (and I have appointed unto my servant Joseph to hold this power in the last days, and there is never but one on the earth at a time on whom this power and the keys of this priesthood are conferred), are of no efficacy, virtue, or force in and after the resurrection from the dead; for all contracts that are not made unto this end have an end when men are dead.

8 Behold, mine house is a house of order, saith the Lord God, and not a house of confusion.

9 Will I accept of an offering, saith the Lord, that is not made in my name?

10 Or will I receive at your hands that which I have not appointed?

11 And will I appoint unto you, saith the Lord, except it be by law, even as I and my Father ordained unto you, before the world was?

12 I am the Lord thy God; and I give unto you this commandment—that no man shall come unto the Father but by me or by my word, which is my law, saith the Lord.

13 And everything that is in the world, whether it be ordained of men, by thrones, or principalities, or powers, or things of name, whatsoever they may be, that are not by me or by my word, saith the Lord, shall be thrown down, and shall not remain after men are dead, neither in nor after the resurrection, saith the Lord your God.

14 For whatsoever things remain are by me; and whatsoever things are not by me shall be shaken and destroyed.

15 Therefore, if a man marry him a wife in the world, and he marry her not by me nor by my word, and he covenant with her so long as he is in the world and she with him, their covenant and marriage are not of force when they are dead, and when they are out of the world; therefore, they are not bound by any law when they are out of the world.

16 Therefore, when they are out of the world they neither marry nor are given in marriage; but are appointed angels in heaven, which angels are ministering servants, to minister for those who are worthy of a far more, and an exceeding, and an eternal weight of glory.

17 For these angels did not abide my law; therefore, they cannot be enlarged, but remain separately and singly, without exaltation, in their saved condition, to all eternity; and from henceforth are not gods, but are angels of God forever and ever.

18 And again, verily I say unto you, if a man marry a wife, and make a covenant with her for time and for all eternity, if that covenant is not by me or by my word, which is my law, and is not sealed by the Holy Spirit of promise, through him whom I have anointed and appointed unto this power, then it is not valid neither of force when they are out of the world, because they are not joined by me, saith the Lord, neither by my word; when they are out of the world it cannot be received there, because the angels and the gods are appointed there, by whom they cannot pass; they cannot, therefore, inherit my glory; for my house is a house of order, saith the Lord God.

19 And again, verily I say unto you, if a man marry a wife by my word, which is my law, and by the new and everlasting covenant, and it is sealed unto them by the Holy Spirit of promise, by him who is anointed, unto whom I have appointed this power and the keys of this priesthood; and it shall be said unto them—Ye shall come forth in the first resurrection; and if it be after the first resurrection, in the next resurrection; and shall inherit thrones,

kingdoms, principalities, and powers, dominions, all heights and depths—then shall it be written in the Lamb's Book of Life, that he shall commit no murder whereby to shed innocent blood, and if ye abide in my covenant, and commit no murder whereby to shed innocent blood, it shall be done unto them in all things whatsoever my servant hath put upon them, in time, and through all eternity; and shall be of full force when they are out of the world; and they shall pass by the angels, and the gods, which are set there, to their exaltation and glory in all things, as hath been sealed upon their heads, which glory shall be a fulness and a continuation of the seeds forever and ever.

20 Then shall they be gods, because they have no end; therefore shall they be from everlasting to everlasting, because they continue; then shall they be above all, because all things are subject unto them. Then shall they be gods, because they have all power, and the angels are subject unto them.

21 Verily, verily, I say unto you, except ye abide my law ye cannot attain to this glory.

22 For strait is the gate, and narrow the way that leadeth unto the exaltation and continuation of the lives, and few there be that find it, because ye receive me not in the world neither do ye know me.

23 But if ye receive me in the world, then shall ye know me, and shall receive your exaltation; that where I am ye shall be also.

24 This is eternal lives—to know the only wise and true God, and Jesus Christ, whom he hath sent. I am he. Receive ye, therefore, my law.

25 Broad is the gate, and wide the way that leadeth to the deaths; and many there are that go in thereat, because they receive me not, neither do they abide in my law.

26 Verily, verily, I say unto you, if a man marry a wife according to my word, and they are sealed by the Holy Spirit of promise, according to mine appointment, and he or she shall commit any sin or transgression of the new and everlasting covenant whatever, and all manner of blasphemies, and if they commit no murder wherein they shed innocent blood, yet they shall come

forth in the first resurrection, and enter into their exaltation; but they shall be destroyed in the flesh, and shall be delivered unto the buffetings of Satan unto the day of redemption, saith the Lord God.

27 The blasphemy against the Holy Ghost, which shall not be forgiven in the world nor out of the world, is in that ye commit murder wherein ye shed innocent blood, and assent unto my death, after ye have received my new and everlasting covenant, saith the Lord God; and he that abideth not this law can in nowise enter into my glory, but shall be damned, saith the Lord.

28 I am the Lord thy God, and will give unto thee the law of my Holy Priesthood, as was ordained by me and my Father before the world was.

29 Abraham received all things, whatsoever he received, by revelation and commandment, by my word, saith the Lord, and hath entered into his exaltation and sitteth upon his throne.

30 Abraham received promises concerning his seed, and of the fruit of his loins—from whose loins ye are, namely, my servant Joseph—which were to continue so long as they were in the world; and as touching Abraham and his seed, out of the world they should continue; both in the world and out of the world should they continue as innumerable as the stars; or, if ye were to count the sand upon the seashore ye could not number them.

31 This promise is yours also, because ye are of Abraham, and the promise was made unto Abraham; and by this law is the continuation of the works of my Father, wherein he glorifieth himself.

32 Go ye, therefore, and do the works of Abraham; enter ye into my law and ye shall be saved.

33 But if ye enter not into my law ye cannot receive the promise of my Father, which he made unto Abraham.

34 God commanded Abraham, and Sarah gave Hagar to Abraham to wife. And why did she do it? Because this was the law; and from Hagar sprang many people. This, therefore, was fulfilling, among other things, the promises.

35 Was Abraham, therefore, under condemnation? Verily I say unto you, Nay; for I, the Lord, commanded it.

36 Abraham was commanded to offer his son Isaac; nevertheless, it was written: Thou shalt not kill. Abraham, however, did not refuse, and it was accounted unto him for righteousness.

37 Abraham received concubines, and they bore him children; and it was accounted unto him for righteousness, because they were given unto him, and he abode in my law; as Isaac also and Jacob did none other things than that which they were commanded; and because they did none other things than that which they were commanded, they have entered into their exaltation, according to the promises, and sit upon thrones, and are not angels but are gods.

38 David also received many wives and concubines, and also Solomon and Moses my servants, as also many others of my servants, from the beginning of creation until this time; and in nothing did they sin save in those things which they received not of me.

39 David's wives and concubines were given unto him of me, by the hand of Nathan, my servant, and others of the prophets who had the keys of this power; and in none of these things did he sin against me save in the case of Uriah and his wife; and, therefore he hath fallen from his exaltation, and received his portion; and he shall not inherit them out of the world, for I gave them unto another, saith the Lord.

40 I am the Lord thy God, and I gave unto thee, my servant Joseph, an appointment, and restore all things. Ask what ye will, and it shall be given unto you according to my word.

41 And as ye have asked concerning adultery, verily, verily, I say unto you, if a man receiveth a wife in the new and everlasting covenant, and if she be with another man, and I have not appointed unto her by the holy anointing, she hath committed adultery and shall be destroyed.

42 If she be not in the new and everlasting covenant, and she be with another man, she has committed adultery.

43 And if her husband be with another woman, and he was under a vow, he hath broken his vow and hath committed adultery.

44 And if she hath not committed adultery, but is innocent and hath not broken her vow, and she knoweth it, and I reveal it unto you, my servant Joseph, then shall you have power, by the power of my Holy Priesthood, to take her and give her unto him that hath not committed adultery but hath been faithful; for he shall be made ruler over many.

45 For I have conferred upon you the keys and power of the priesthood, wherein I restore all things, and make known unto you all things in due time.

46 And verily, verily, I say unto you, that whatsoever you seal on earth shall be sealed in heaven; and whatsoever you bind on earth, in my name and by my word, saith the Lord, it shall be eternally bound in the heavens; and whosesoever sins you remit on earth shall be remitted eternally in the heavens; and whosesoever sins you retain on earth shall be retained in heaven.

47 And again, verily I say, whomsoever you bless I will bless, and whomsoever you curse I will curse, saith the Lord; for I, the Lord, am thy God.

48 And again, verily I say unto you, my servant Joseph, that whatsoever you give on earth, and to whomsoever you give any one on earth, by my word and according to my law, it shall be visited with blessings and not cursings, and with my power, saith the Lord, and shall be without condemnation on earth and in heaven.

49 For I am the Lord thy God, and will be with thee even unto the end of the world, and through all eternity; for verily I seal upon you your exaltation, and prepare a throne for you in the kingdom of my Father, with Abraham your father.

50 Behold, I have seen your sacrifices, and will forgive all your sins; I have seen your sacrifices in obedience to that which I have told you. Go,

therefore, and I make a way for your escape, as I accepted the offering of Abraham of his son Isaac.

51 Verily, I say unto you: A commandment I give unto mine handmaid, Emma Smith, your wife, whom I have given unto you, that she stay herself and partake not of that which I commanded you to offer unto her; for I did it, saith the Lord, to prove you all, as I did Abraham, and that I might require an offering at your hand, by covenant and sacrifice.

52 And let mine handmaid, Emma Smith, receive all those that have been given unto my servant Joseph, and who are virtuous and pure before me; and those who are not pure, and have said they were pure, shall be destroyed, saith the Lord God.

53 For I am the Lord thy God and ye shall obey my voice; and I give unto my servant Joseph that he shall be made ruler over many things; for he hath been faithful over a few things, and from henceforth I will strengthen him.

54 And I command mine handmaid, Emma Smith, to abide and cleave unto my servant Joseph, and to none else. But if she will not abide this commandment she shall be destroyed, saith the Lord; for I am the Lord thy God, and will destroy her if she abide not in my law.

55 But if she will not abide this commandment, then shall my servant Joseph do all things for her, even as he hath said; and I will bless him and multiply him and give unto him an hundredfold in this world, of fathers and mothers, brothers and sisters, houses and lands, wives and children, and crowns of eternal lives in the eternal worlds.

56 And again, verily I say, let mine handmaid forgive my servant Joseph his trespasses; and then shall she be forgiven her trespasses, wherein she has trespassed against me; and I, the Lord thy God, will bless her, and multiply her, and make her heart to rejoice.

57 And again, I say, let not my servant Joseph put his property out of his hands, lest an enemy come and destroy him; for Satan seeketh to destroy; for

I am the Lord thy God, and he is my servant; and behold, and lo, I am with him, as I was with Abraham, thy father, even unto his exaltation and glory.

58 Now, as touching the law of the priesthood, there are many things pertaining thereunto.

59 Verily, if a man be called of my Father, as was Aaron, by mine own voice, and by the voice of him that sent me, and I have endowed him with the keys of the power of this priesthood, if he do anything in my name, and according to my law and by my word, he will not commit sin, and I will justify him.

60 Let no one, therefore, set on my servant Joseph; for I will justify him; for he shall do the sacrifice which I require at his hands for his transgressions, saith the Lord your God.

61 And again, as pertaining to the law of the priesthood—if any man espouse a virgin, and desire to espouse another, and the first give her consent, and if he espouse the second, and they are virgins, and have vowed to no other man, then is he justified; he cannot commit adultery for they are given unto him; for he cannot commit adultery with that that belongeth unto him and to no one else.

62 And if he have ten virgins given unto him by this law, he cannot commit adultery, for they belong to him, and they are given unto him; therefore is he justified.

63 But if one or either of the ten virgins, after she is espoused, shall be with another man, she has committed adultery, and shall be destroyed; for they are given unto him to multiply and replenish the earth, according to my commandment, and to fulfil the promise which was given by my Father before the foundation of the world, and for their exaltation in the eternal worlds, that they may bear the souls of men; for herein is the work of my Father continued, that he may be glorified.

64 And again, verily, verily, I say unto you, if any man have a wife, who holds the keys of this power, and he teaches unto her the law of my priest-

hood, as pertaining to these things, then shall she believe and administer unto him, or she shall be destroyed, saith the Lord your God; for I will destroy her; for I will magnify my name upon all those who receive and abide in my law.

65 Therefore, it shall be lawful in me, if she receive not this law, for him to receive all things whatsoever I, the Lord his God, will give unto him, because she did not believe and administer unto him according to my word; and she then becomes the transgressor; and he is exempt from the law of Sarah, who administered unto Abraham according to the law when I commanded Abraham to take Hagar to wife.

66 And now, as pertaining to this law, verily, verily, I say unto you, I will reveal more unto you, hereafter; therefore, let this suffice for the present. Behold, I am Alpha and Omega. Amen.

Appendix B

THE RULES OF PLURAL MARRIAGE

The Rules of Plural Marriage written by Orson Pratt, taken from *The Seer*, vol 1:11&12, Nov. & Dec. 1853

Nothing is so much to be desired in families as peace, love, and union: they are essential to happiness here and hereafter. And, in order to promote these desirable objects, we would recommend the observance of the following rules.

Rule 1st

Let that man who intends to become a husband, seek first the kingdom of God and its righteousness, and learn to govern himself, according to the law of God: for he that cannot govern himself cannot govern others: let him dedicate his property, his talents, his time, and even his life to the service of God, holding all things at His disposal, to do with the same, according as He shall direct through the counsel that He has ordained.

Rule 2nd

Let him next seek for wisdom to direct him in the choice of his wives. Let him seek for those whose qualifications will render him and themselves happy. Let him look not wholly at the beauty of the countenance, or the splendor of the apparel, or the great fortune, or the artful smiles, or the affected modesty of females; for all these, without the genuine virtues, are like the dew-drops which glitter for a moment in the sun, and dazzle the eye, but soon vanish away. But let him look for kind and amiable dispositions; for unaffected modesty; for industrious habits; for sterling virtue; for honesty, integrity, and truthfulness; for cleanliness in persons, in apparel, in cooking, and in every kind of domestic labor; for cheerfulness, patience, and stability of character; and above all, for genuine religion to control and govern their every thought and deed. When he has found those possessing these qualifications let him seek to obtain them lawfully through the counsel of him who holds the keys of the everlasting priesthood, that they may be married to him by the authority of Heaven, and thus be secured to him for time and for all eternity.

Rule 3rd

When a man has obtained his wives, let him not suppose that they are already perfect in all things; for this cannot be expected in those who are young and inexperienced in the cares and vicissitudes of a married life. They, as weaker vessels, are given to him as the stronger, to nourish, cherish, and protect; to be their head, their patriarch, and their saviour; to teach, instruct, counsel, and perfect them in all things relating to family government, and the welfare and happiness of themselves and their children. Therefore, let him realize the weighty responsibility now placed upon him, as the head of a family; and also let him study diligently the disposition of his wives, that he may know how to instruct them in wisdom for their good.

Rule 4th

Betray not the confidence of your wives. There are many ideas in an affectionate confiding wife which she would wish to communicate to her husband, and yet she would be very unwilling to have them communicated to others. Keep each of your wives' secrets from all the others, and from any one else, unless in cases where good will result by doing otherwise.

Rule 5th

Speak not of the faults of your wives to others; for in so doing, you speak against yourself. If you speak to one of your wives of the imperfections of the others who may be absent, you not only injure them in her estimation, but she will expect that you will speak against her under like circumstances: this is calculated to weaken their confidence in you, and sow division in the family. Tell each one of her faults in private in a spirit of kindness and love, and she will most probably respect you for it, and endeavor to do better for the future; and thus the others will not, because of your reproof, take occasion to speak reproachfully of her. There may be circumstances, when reproof, given in the presence of the others, will produce a salutary influence upon all. Wisdom is profitable to direct, and should be sought for earnestly by those who have the responsibility of families.

Rule 6th

Avoid anger and a fretful peevish disposition in your family. A hasty spirit, accompanied with harsh words, will most generally beget its own likeness, or, at least, it will, eventually, sour the feelings of your wives and children, and greatly weaken their affections for you. You should remember that harsh expressions against one of your wives, used in the hearing of the others, will more deeply wound her feelings, than if she alone heard them. Reproofs that are timely and otherwise good, may lose their good effect by being administered in a wrong spirit, indeed, they will most probably increase the evils which they were intended to remedy. Do not find fault with every trifling error that you may see; for this will discourage your family, and they will begin to think that it is impossible to please you; and, after a while, become indifferent as to whether they please you or not. How unhappy and extremely wretched is that family where nothing pleases—where scolding has become almost as natural as breathing!

Rule 7th

Use impartiality in your family as far as circumstances will allow; and let your kindness and love abound towards them all. Use your own judgment, as the head of the family, in regard to your duties in relation to them, and be not swayed from that which is right, by your own feelings, nor by the feelings of others.

Rule 8th

Suffer not your judgment to be biased against any one of your wives, by the accusations of the others unless you have good grounds to believe that those accusations are just. Decide not hastily upon partial evidence, but weigh well all things, that your mind may not become unjustly prejudiced. When one of your wives complains of the imperfections of the others, and endeavors to set your mind against them, teach her that all have imperfections, and of the necessity of bearing one with another in patience, and of praying one for another.

Rule 9th

Call your wives and children together frequently, and instruct them in their duties towards God, towards yourself, and towards one another. Pray with them and for them often; and teach them to pray much, that the Holy Spirit may dwell in their midst, without which it is impossible to maintain that union, love, and oneness which are so necessary to happiness and salvation.

Rule 10th

Remember, that notwithstanding written rules will be of service in teaching you your duties, as the head of a family, yet without the Holy Ghost to teach and instruct you, it is impossible for you to govern a family in righteousness; therefore, seek after the Holy Ghost and He shall teach you all things, and sanctify you and your family, and make you one, that you may be perfected in Him and He in you, and eventually be exalted on high to dwell with God, where your joy will be full forever.

Rule 11th

Let no woman unite herself in marriage with any man, unless she has fully resolved to submit herself wholly to his counsel, and to let him govern as the head. It is far better for her not to be united with him in the sacred bonds of eternal union, than to rebel against the divine order of family government, instituted for a higher salvation; for if she altogether turn therefrom, she will receive a greater condemnation.

Rule 12th

Never seek to prejudice the mind of your husband against any of his other wives, for the purpose of exalting yourself in his estimation, lest the evil which you unjustly try to bring upon them, fall with double weight upon your own head. Strive to rise in favor and influence with your husband by your own merits, and not by magnifying the faults of others.

Rule 13th

Seek to be a peacemaker in the family with whom you are associated. If you see the least appearance of division arising, use your utmost efforts to restore union and soothe the feelings of all. Soft and gentle words, spoken in season, will allay contention and strife; while a hasty spirit and harsh language add fuel to the fire already kindled which will rage with increasing violence.

Rule 14th

Speak not evil of your husband unto any of the rest of the family for the purpose of prejudicing their minds against him; for if he be informed thereof, it will injure you in his estimation. Neither speak evil of any members of the family; for this will destroy their confidence in you. Avoid all hypocracy; for if you pretend to love your husband and to honor and respect his wives, when present, but speak disrespectful of them when absent, you will be looked upon as a hypocrite, as a tattler, and as a mischief-making woman, and be shunned as being more dangerous than an open enemy.

And what is still more detestable, is to tattle out of the family, and endeavor to create enemies against those with whom you are connected. Such persons should not only be considered hypocrites, but traitors, and their conduct should be despised by every lover of righteousness. Remember also, that there are more ways than one to tattle; it is not always the case that those persons who are the boldest in their accusations that are the most dangerous slanderers; but such as hypocritically pretend that they do not wish to injure their friends, and at the same time, very piously insinuate in dark indirect sayings, something that is calculated to leave a very unfavorable prejudice against them. Shun such a spirit as you would the very gates of hell.

Rule 15th

If you see any of your husband's wives sick or in trouble, use every effort to relieve them, and to administer kindness and consolations, remembering that you, yourself, under the same circumstances, would be thankful for their assistance. Endeavor to share each others burdens, according to the health, ability, and strength which God has given you. Do not be afraid that you will do more than your share of the domestic labor, or that you will be more kind to them than they are to you.

Rule 16th

Let each mother correct her own children, and see that they do not dispute and quarrel with each other, nor with any others; let her not correct the children of the others without liberty so to do, lest it give offence. The husband should see that each mother maintains a wise and proper discipline over her children, especially in their younger years: and it is his duty to see that all of his children are obedient to himself and to their respective mothers. And it is also his duty to see that the children of one wife are not allowed to quarrel and abuse those of the others, neither to be disrespectful or impudent to any branch of his family.

Rule 17th

It is the duty of parents to instruct their children, according to their capacities in every principle of the gospel, as revealed in the Book of Mormon and in the revelations which God has given, that they may grow up in righteousness, and in the fear of the Lord, and have faith in Him. Suffer no wickedness to have place among them, but teach them the right way, and see that they walk therein. And let the husband, and his wives, and all of his children that have come to the years of understanding. often bow before the Lord around the family altar, and pray vocally and unitedly for whatever blessings they stand in need of, remembering that where there are union and peace, there will also be faith, and hope, and the love of God, and every good work, and a multiplicity of blessings, imparting health and comfort to the body, and joy and life to the soul.

Rule 18th

Let each mother commence with her children when young, not only to teach and instruct them, but to chasten and bring them into the most perfect subjection; for then is the time that they are the most easily conquered, and their tender minds are the most susceptible of influences and government. Many mothers from carelessness neglect their children, and only attempt to govern them at long intervals, when they most generally find their efforts of no lasting benefit; for the children having been accustomed to have their own way, do not easily yield; and if peradventure they do yield, it is only for the time being, until the mother relaxes again into carelessness, when they return again to their accustomed habits: and thus by habit they become more and more confirmed in disobedience, waxing worse and worse, until the mother becomes discouraged, and relinquishes all discipline, and complains that she cannot make her children mind. The fault is not so much in the children, as in the carelessness and neglect of the mother when the children were young; it is she that must answer, in a great degree, for the evil habits and disobedience of the children. She is more directly responsible than the father; for it cannot be expected that the father can always find time, apart from the laborious duties required of him, to correct and manage his little children who are at home with their mothers.

It is frequently the case that the father is called to attend to duties in public life, and may be absent from home much of his time, when the whole duty of family government necessarily rests upon the respective mothers of his children; if they, through carelessness, suffer their children to grow up in disobedience and ruin themselves, they must bear the shame and disgrace thereof.

Some mothers, though not careless, and though they feel the greatest anxiety for the welfare of their children, yet, through a mistaken notion of love for them, forbear to punish them when they need punishment, or if they undertake to conquer them, their tenderness and pity are so great, that they prevail over the judgment, and the children are left unconquered, and become more determined to resist all future efforts of their mothers until, at length, they conclude that their children have a more stubborn disposition than others, and that it is impossible to subject them in obedience. In this case, as in that of neglect, the fault is the mothers.

The stubbornness of the children, for the most part, is the effect of the mother's indulgence, arising from her mistaken idea of love. By that which she calls love, she ruins her children. Children between one and two years of age are capable of being made to understand many things; then is the time to begin with them. How often we see children of that age manifest much anger. Frequently by crying through anger, they that are otherwise healthy, injure themselves: it is far better, in such instances, for a mother to correct her child in a gentle manner though with decision and firmness until she conquers it, and causes it to cease crying, than to suffer that habit to increase. When the child by gentle punishment has learned this one lesson from its mother, it is much more easily conquered and brought into subjection in other things, until finally, by a little perseverance on the part of the mother, it learns to be obedient to her voice in all things; and obedience becomes confirmed into a permanent habit.

Such a child trained by a negligent or overindulgent mother, might have become confirmed in habits of stubbornness and disobedience. It is not so much in the original constitution of children as in their training, that causes such wide differences in their dispositions. It cannot be denied, that there is a difference in the constitution of children even from their birth; but this difference is mostly owing to the proper or improper conduct of parents, as before stated; therefore, even for this difference, parents are more or less responsible.

If parents, through their own evil conduct entail hereditary dispositions upon their children which are calculated to ruin them, unless properly curtailed and overcome, they should realize, that for that evil they must render an account. If parents have been guilty in entailing upon their offspring unhappy dispositions, let them repent, by using all diligence to save them from the evil consequences which will naturally result by giving way to those dispositions. The greater the derangement, the greater must be the remedy, and the more skilful and thorough should be its application, until that which is sown in evil is overcome and completely subdued. In this way parents may save themselves and their children; but otherwise there is condemnation. Therefore, we repeat again, let mothers begin to discipline their children when young.

Rule 19th

Do not correct children in anger; an angry parent is not as well prepared to judge of the amount of punishment which should be inflicted upon a child, as one that is more cool and exercised with reflection, reason, and judgment. Let your children see that you punish them, not to gratify an angry disposition, but to reform them for their good, and it will have a salutary influence; they will not look upon you as a tyrant, swayed to and fro by turbulent and furious passions; but they will regard you as one that seeks their welfare, and that you only chasten them because you love them, and wish them to do well. Be deliberate and calm in your counsels and reproofs, but at the same time use earnestness and decision. Let your children know that your words must be respected and obeyed.

Rule 20th

Never deceive your children by threatnings or promises. Be careful not to threaten them with a punishment which you have no intention of inflicting; for this will cause them to lose confidence in your word; besides, it will cause them to contract the habit of lying: when they perceive that their parents do not fulfil their threatenings or promises, they will consider that there is no harm in forfeiting their word. Think not that your precepts, concerning truthfulness, will have much weight upon the minds of your children, when they are contradicted by your examples. Be careful to fulfil your word in all things in righteousness, and your children will not only learn to be truthful from your example, but they will fear to disobey your word, knowing that you never fail to punish or reward according to your threatnings and promises. Let your laws, penalties, and rewards be founded upon the principles of justice and mercy, and adapted to the capacities of your children; for this is the way that our heavenly Father governs His children, giving to some a Celestial; to others a Terrestrial; and to others still a Telestial law, with penalties and promises annexed, according to the conditions, circumstances, and capacities of the individuals to be governed. Seek for wisdom and pattern after the heavenly order of government.

Rule 21st

Do not be so stern and rigid in your family government as to render yourself an object of fear and dread. There are parents who only render themselves conspicuous in the attribute of Justice, while mercy and love are scarcely known in their families. Justice should be tempered with mercy, and love should be the great moving principle, interweaving itself in all your family administrations.

When justice alone sits upon the throne, your children approach you with dread, or peradventure hide themselves from your presence, and long for your absence that they may be relieved from their fear; at the sound of your approaching foot-steps they flee as from an enemy, and tremble at your voice, and shrink from the gaze of your countenance, as though they expected some terrible punishment to be inflicted upon them. Be familiar with your children that they may delight themselves in your society, and look upon you as a kind and tender parent whom they delight to obey.

Obedience inspired by love, and obedience inspired by fear, are entirely different in their nature; the former will be permanent and enduring, while the latter only waits to have the object of fear removed, and it vanishes like a dream. Govern children as parents, and not as tyrants; for they will be parents in their turn, and will be very likely to adopt that form of government in which they have been educated. If you have been tyrants, they may be influenced to pattern after your example. If you are fretful and continually scolding, they will be very apt to be scolds too. If you are loving, kind, and merciful, these benign influences will be very certain to infuse themselves into their order of family government; and thus good and evil influences frequently extend themselves down for many generations and ages. How great, then, are the responsibilities of parents to their children! And how fearful the consequences of bad examples! Let love, therefore, predominate and control you, and your children will be sure to discover it, and will love you in return.

Rule 22nd

Let each mother teach her children to honor and love their father, and to respect his teachings and counsels. How frequently it is the case, when fathers undertake to correct their children, mothers will interfere in the presence of the children: this has a very evil tendency in many respects: first, it destroys the oneness of feeling which should exist between husband and wife; secondly, it weakens the confidence of the children in the father, and emboldens them to disobedience; thirdly, it creates strife and discord; and lastly, it is rebelling against the order of family government, established by divine wisdom.

If the mother supposes the father too severe, let her not mention this in the presence of the children, but she can express her feelings to him while alone by themselves, and thus the children will not see any division between them. For husband and wives to be disagreed, and to contend, and quarrel, is a great evil; and to do these things in the presence of their children, is a still greater evil. Therefore, if a husband and his wives will quarrel and destroy their own happiness, let them have pity upon their children, and not destroy them by their pernicious examples.

Rule 23rd

Suffer not children of different mothers to be haughty and abusive to each other; for they are own brothers and sisters the same as the children of the patriarch Jacob; and one has no claim above another, only as his conduct merits it. Should you discover contentions or differences arising, do not justify your own children and condemn the others in their presence; for this will encourage them in their quarrels: even if you consider that your children are not so much in the fault as the others, it is far better to teach them of the evils of strife, than to speak against the others. To speak against them, not only alienates their affections, but has a tendency to offend their mothers, and create unpleasant feelings between you and them.

Always speak well of each of your husband's wives in the presence of your children; for children generally form their judgment concerning others, by the sayings of their parents: they are very apt to respect those whom their parents respect; and hate those whom they hate. If you consider that some of the mothers are too lenient with their children and too negligent in correcting them, do not be offended, but strive, by the wise and prudent management of your own, to set a worthy example before them, that they, by seeing your judicious and wise course, may be led to go and do likewise. Examples will sometimes reform, when precepts fail.

Rule 24th

Be industrious in your habits: this is important as fulfilling the law of God: it is also important for those who are in low circumstances, that they may acquire food, and raiment, and the necessary comforts of life: it is also important for the rich as well as the poor, that they may be able more abundantly to supply the wants of the needy, and be in circumstances to help the unfortunate and administer to the sick and afflicted; for in this way, it is possible even for the rich to enter into the kingdom of heaven. A family whose time is occupied in the useful and lawful avocations of life, will find no time to go from house to house, tattling and injuring one another and their neighbors; neither will they be so apt to quarrel among themselves.

Rule 25th

When your children are from three to five years of age, send them to school, and keep them there year after year until they receive a thorough education in all the rudiments of useful science, and in their manners, and morals. In this manner, they will avoid many evils, arising from indolence, and form habits that will render them beneficial to society in after life. Let mothers educate their daughters in all kinds of domestic labor: teach them to wash and iron, to bake and do all kinds of cooking, to knit and sew, to spin and weave, and to do all other things that will qualify them to be good and efficient housewives.

Let fathers educate their sons in whatever branch or branches of business, they intend them respectively to follow. Despise that false delicacy which is exhibited by the sons and daughters of the rich, who consider it a dishonor to labor at the common avocations of life. Such notions of high-life, should be frowned out of the territory, as too contemptible to be harbored, for one moment, by a civilized community. Some of these bogus gentlemen and ladies have such grand ideas, concerning gentility, that they would let their poor old father and mother slave themselves to death, to support them in their idleness, or at some useless fanciful employment.

The daughter will sit down in the parlour at her painting or music, arrayed in silks and fineries, and let her mother wash and cook until, through fatigue, she is ready to fall into her grave: this they call gentility, and the distinctions between the low and the high. But such daughters are not worthy of husbands, and should not be admitted into any respectable society: they are contemptible drones, that would be a curse to any husband who should be so unfortunate as to be connected with such nuisances. Painting, music, and all the fine arts, should be cherished, and cultivated, as accomplishments which serve to adorn and embellish an enlightened civilized people, and render life agreeable and happy; but when these are cultivated, to the exclusion of the more necessary duties and qualifications, it is like adorning swine with costly jewels and pearls to make them appear more respectable: these embellishments, only render such characters a hundred fold more odious and disgustful than they would otherwise appear.

Rule 26th

Use economy and avoid wastefulness. How discouraging it would be to a husband who has a large family, depending mostly upon his labor for a support, to see his wives and children carelessly, thoughtlessly, and unnecessarily, waste his hard earnings. Let not one wife, for fear that she shall not obtain her share of the income, destroy, give away, and otherwise foolishly dispose of what is given to her, thinking that her husband will furnish her with more. Those who economize and wisely use that which is given to them, should be counted worthy to receive more abundantly than those who pursue a contrary course. Each wife should feel interested in saving and preserving that with which the Lord has entrusted her, and should rejoice, not only in her prosperity, but in the prosperity of all the others: her eyes should not be full of greediness to grasp every thing herself, but she should feel equally interested in the welfare of the whole family. By pursuing this course she will be beloved: by taking a contrary course, she will be considered selfish and little minded.

Rule 27th

Let husbands, wives, sons, and daughters, continually realize that their relationships do not end with this short life, but will continue in eternity without end. Every qualification and disposition therefore, which will render them happy here, should be nourished, cherished, enlarged, and perfected, that their union may be indissoluble, and their happiness secured both for this world and for that which is to come. Let these rules be observed and all others that are good and righteous, and peace will be the result: husbands will be patriarchs and saviours; wives will be like fruitful vines, bringing forth precious fruits in their seasons: their sons will be like plants of renown, and their daughters like the polished stones of a palace.

Then the saints shall flourish upon the hills and rejoice upon the mountains, and become a great people and strong, whose goings forth shall be with strength that is everlasting. Arise, O Zion! clothe thyself with light! shine forth with clearness and brilliancy! illuminate the nations and the dark corners of the earth, for their light is gone out—their sun is set—gross darkness covers them! let thy light be seen upon the high places of the earth; let it shine in glorious splendour; for then shall the wicked see, and be confounded, and lay their hands upon their mouths in shame; then shall kings arise, and come forth to the light, and rejoice in the greatness of thy glory! Fear not, O Zion, nor let thine hands be slack, for great is the Holy One in the midst of thee! a cloud shall be over thee by day for a defense, and at night thy dwellings shall be encircled with glory! God is thine everlasting light, and shall be a Tower of strength against thine enemies; at the sound of His voice they shall melt away, and terrors shall seize upon them.

In that day thou shalt be beautiful and glorious, and the reproach of the Gentiles shall no more come into thine ears; in that day, shall the sons of them that afflicted thee come bending unto thee and bow themselves down at the soles of thy feet; and the daughters of them that reproached thee, shall come, saying, We will eat our own bread and wear our own apparel, only let us be joined in the patriarchal order of marriage with the husbands and patriarchs in Zion to take away our reproach: then shall they highly esteem, far above riches, that which their wicked fathers ridiculed under the name of Polygamy.

Appendix C

THE FAMILY: A PROCLAMATION TO THE WORLD

Proclamation read by President Gordon B. Hinckley at the
General Relief Society Meeting, September 23, 1995,
Salt Lake City, Utah

We, the First Presidency and the Council of the Twelve Apostles of The Church of Jesus Christ of Latter-day Saints, solemnly proclaim that marriage between a man and a woman is ordained of God and that the family is central to the Creator's plan for the eternal destiny of His children.

All human beings—male and female—are created in the image of God. Each is a beloved spirit son or daughter of heavenly parents, and, as such, each has a divine nature and destiny. Gender is an essential characteristic of individual premortal, mortal, and eternal identity and purpose.

In the premortal realm, spirit sons and daughters knew and worshiped God as their Eternal Father and accepted His plan by which His children could obtain a physical body and gain earthly experience to progress toward perfection and ultimately realize his or her divine destiny as an heir of eternal life. The divine plan of happiness enables family relationships to be perpetuated beyond the grave. Sacred ordinances and covenants available in holy temples make it possible for individuals to return to the presence of God and for families to be united eternally.

The first commandment that God gave to Adam and Eve pertained to their potential for parenthood as husband and wife. We declare that God's commandment for His children to multiply and replenish the earth remains in force. We further declare that God has commanded that the sacred powers of procreation are to be employed only between man and woman, lawfully wedded as husband and wife.

We declare the means by which mortal life is created to be divinely appointed. We affirm the sanctity of life and of its importance in God's eternal plan.

Husband and wife have a solemn responsibility to love and care for each other and for their children. "Children are an heritage of the Lord" (Psalms 127:3). Parents have a sacred duty to rear their children in love and righteousness, to provide for their physical and spiritual needs, to teach them to love and serve one another, to observe the commandments of God and to be law-abiding citizens wherever they live. Husbands and wives—mothers and fathers—will be held accountable before God for the discharge of these obligations.

The family is ordained of God. Marriage between man and woman is essential to His eternal plan. Children are entitled to birth within the bonds of matrimony, and to be reared by a father and a mother who honor marital vows with complete fidelity. Happiness in family life is most likely to be achieved when founded upon the teachings of the Lord Jesus Christ. Successful marriages and families are established and maintained on principles of faith, prayer, repentance, forgiveness, respect, love, compassion, work, and wholesome recreational activities. By divine design, fathers are to preside over their families in love and righteousness and are responsible to provide the necessities of life and protection for their families. Mothers are primarily responsible for the nurture of their children. In these sacred responsibilities, fathers and mothers are obligated to help one another as equal partners. Disability, death, or other circumstances may necessitate individual adaptation. Extended families should lend support when needed.

We warn that individuals who violate covenants of chastity, who abuse spouse or offspring, or who fail to fulfill family responsibilities will one day stand accountable before God. Further, we warn that the disintegration of the family will bring upon individuals, communities, and nations the calamities foretold by ancient and modern prophets.

We call upon responsible citizens and officers of government everywhere to promote those measures designed to maintain and strengthen the family as the fundamental unit of society.

~ The First Presidency and Council of the Twelve Apostles of The Church of Jesus Christ of Latter-day Saints

End Notes

Chapter One
1. Helen M. Callister, Papers, (ca. 1878), Church Archives, Church of Jesus Christ of Latter-day Saints, Salt Lake City, UT, (hereafter cited as Church Archives).
2. Gordon B. Hinckley, *Standing For Something*, (Times Books, New York, 2000), p. 104.

Chapter Two
1. Joseph Fielding Smith, *Teachings of the Prophet Joseph Smith*, (Deseret Book Company, Salt Lake City, UT, 1938), p. 332.
2. William Clayton, Letter Salt Lake City to Madison M. Scott 1871 Nov. 11, Church Archives.
3. Doctrine and Covenants, Church of Jesus Christ of Latter-day Saints, Salt Lake City, UT (hereafter cited as D&C).
4. Eliza R. Snow, Historical Record, Church Archives, vol. 6, p. 224.
5. Linda King Newell and Valeen Tippetts Avery, *Mormon Enigma: Emma Hale Smith*, (Doubleday & Company, Inc., Garden City, New York, 1984), p. 145.
6. Emma Hale Smith, Blessing (1844), Church Archives.
7. Gracia N. Jones, *Emma and Joseph: Their Divine Mission*, (Covenant Communications Inc., American Fork, UT, 1999), p. 343.
8. Statement of Mrs. L.W. Kimball (n.d.), Church Archives (minor spelling corrections, paragraphing added).
9. Eliza R. Snow Smith, *Biography and Family Record of Lorenzo Snow*, (Deseret News Company, Printers 1884, Salt Lake City, UT), p. 68 (paragraphing added).
10. Samuel Claridge, Autobiography (ca. 1910), Church Archives.

11. B.H. Roberts, *Comprehensive History of the Church*, 6 vols., (Church of Jesus Christ of Latter-day Saints, Salt Lake City, UT, 1930), vol. 2, p. 103.
12. Testimony of Sister M. Isabella Horne, 1905, Church Archives.
13. *Ibid.*, (minor spelling corrections, punctuation and paragraphing added).
14. *LDS Biographical Encyclopedia*, ed. Andrew Jenson, 4 vols., (Andrew Jenson History Company, Salt Lake City, UT, 1901), vol. 1, p. 811.
15. *Journal of Discourses*, 26 vols., (London: Latter-day Saints' Book Depot, 1854-1886), (hereafter cited as *Journal of Discourses*), sermon by Brigham Young, vol. 6, p. 281.

CHAPTER THREE

1. Statement of Mrs. L.W. Kimball (n.d.), Church Archives, ("He" is inserted and refers to Heber C. Kimball).
2. Martin Benjamin Bushman, Autobiographical sketch, 1925, Church Archives.
3. Samuel Claridge, Autobiography (ca.1910), Church Archives.
4. Helen Mar Whitney, "Why We Practice Plural Marriage", *Juvenile Instructor*, Salt Lake City, UT, 1884.
5. Christopher J. Arthur, Kimball Young Collection, Special Collections, Harold B. Lee Library, Brigham Young University, Provo, UT (hereafter cited as Kimball Young Collection).
6. Elizabeth Acord Beck, Kimball Young Collection.
7. Miles Edgar Johnson, Autobiography, 1933, Church Archives.
8. Barbara Smith Amussen, Kimball Young Collection.
9. Mary Ann Price Hyde, Reminiscence (ca. 1880), Church Archives.
10. Elizabeth Whitney Autobiography, *Woman's Exponent*, Church Archives, vol. 7, p. 105.
11. Benjamin F. Johnson Letter to George F. Gibbs, 1903, Benjamin Johnson File, Church Archives.
12. Joseph C. Bentley, Kimball Young Collection.
13. Kate Carter, *Daughters of Utah Pioneers Collection*, 17 vols., Salt Lake City, UT, 1968, (hereafter cited as DUP), *Our Pioneer Heritage*, vol. 5, pp. 175-179 (paragraphing added).

14. History of Elizabeth Mears Hawkins Mortensen, (ca. 1972), Church Archives.
15. George Darling Watt, Letter (ca. 1859) to Elizabeth (Golightly), Church Archives (minor spelling corrections).
16. Kate Carter, DUP, *Our Pioneer Heritage*, vol. 1, pp. 387-388.
17. Jane T. Bleak, Kimball Young Collection.
18. Nevada Dansie, "Pioneer Journals" 1997, p. 2, on-line, Internet, Aug. 31, 2001, http://members.tripod.com/~nev7/.
19. Kate Carter, DUP, *Our Pioneer Heritage*, vol. 3, pp. 200-203 (paragraphing added).
20. David King Udall, *Arizona Pioneer Mormon: David King Udall His Story and His Family*, (Arizona Silhouettes, Tucson, AZ, 1959), pp. 97-103.
21. Kate Carter, DUP, *Our Pioneer Heritage*, vol. 17, p. 218.
22 William Hyde, Marriage proposals. Letters 1843–1859, Church Archives (minor spelling corrections, paragraphing added).
23. *LDS Biographical Encyclopedia*, ed. Andrew Jenson, 4 vols., (Andrew Jenson History Company, Salt Lake City, UT, 1901), vol. 1, p. 156 (paragraphing added).
24. Orson Smith, Kimball Young Collection.
25. *Journal of Discourses*, sermon by George Teasdale, vol. 25, p. 21 (paragraphing added).
26. Helen Mar Whitney, "Why We Practice Plural Marriage", *Juvenile Instructor*, Salt Lake City, UT, 1884.

Chapter Four

1. Bathsheba Smith Autobiography, typescript; Special Collections, Harold B. Lee Library, Brigham Young University, Provo, UT, (hereafter cited as Special Collections, BYU), pp. 11-12.
2. Anson B. Call, Kimball Young Collection.
3. John Brown, Kimball Young Collection (minor spelling corrections, paragraphing added).
4. Biographical sketch of Margaret Thompson Smoot, n.d., Church Archives.

5. *Journal of Discourses*, sermon by Elder H. W. Naisbitt, vol. 26, p. 114 (minor spelling corrections, punctuation and paragraphing added).
6. John H. Bott, Kimball Young Collection.
7. Kate Carter, DUP, *Our Pioneer Heritage*, vol. 17, pp. 224-231.
8. Belinda Marden Pratt, "Defense of Polygamy by a Lady of Utah", *Millennial Star*, Salt Lake City, UT, July 29, 1854.
9. Kate Carter, DUP, *Our Pioneer Heritage*, vol. 5, p. 211.
10. Kate Carter, DUP, *Treasures of Pioneer History*, vol. 6, pp. 198-218.
11. Margaret T. Smoot, "'Mormon' Women on Plural Marriage", Nov. 16, 1878, Special Collections, BYU.
12. Statement of Mrs. L.W. Kimball (n.d.), Church Archives (minor spelling corrections, punctuation and paragraphing added).
13. Kate Carter, DUP, *Treasures of Pioneer History*, vol. 6, pp. 222-226.
14. Kate Carter, DUP, *Our Pioneer Heritage*, vol. 5, pp. 264-268 (paragraphing altered).
15. Price Nelson, Kimball Young Collection.
16. Kate Carter, DUP, *An Enduring Legacy*, vol. 7, pp. 80-81.
17. Rozalia Payne, Kimball Young Collection.
18. Lucy Payne, Kimball Young Collection.
19. Ronald Bruce McIntire, with David L. Zolman, *Mary Luella Abbott Leavitt (1865 – 1955)*, (Lincoln Press, Salt Lake City, UT 1997), pp. 107–110 (minor spelling and punctuation corrections).
20. Benjamin F. Johnson Letter to George F. Gibbs, 1903, Benjamin Johnson File, Church Archives.
21. Kate Carter, DUP, *Our Pioneer Heritage*, vol. 15, pp. 239-240.
22. Warren Foote Autobiography, typescript, Special Collections, BYU, p. 64.
23. Joseph C. Bentley, Kimball Young Collection.
24. Helen Mar Whitney, "Why We Practice Plural Marriage", *Juvenile Instructor*, Salt Lake City, UT, 1884.
25. Phoebe Woodruff, "'Mormon' Women on Plural Marriage", Nov. 16, 1878, Special Collections, BYU.
26. Kate Carter, DUP *Our Pioneer Heritage*, vol. 10, p. 84.
27. *Ibid.*, vol. 19, pp. 289-313.
28. John S. Stucki, Kimball Young Collection (minor spelling corrections).

29. Bathsheba Smith Autobiography, typescript, Special Collections, BYU, pp. 11-12.

CHAPTER FIVE
1. Louis Orson Brandley, Interview, Raymond, Alberta, Canada, 1975–1981, Church Archives.
2. Kate Carter, DUP, *Heart Throbs of the West*, vol. 1, pp. 291-292.
3. *Ibid.*, p. 289.
4. *Ibid.*, p. 295 (minor spelling corrections, paragraphing added).
5. Biographical sketch of Thomas Chamberlain, Jr., 1954, Church Archives (minor punctuation corrections, paragraphing added).
6. History of Byron Harvey Allred, Sr., 1960, Church Archives.
7. John Bowen, Kimball Young Collection.
8. Kate Carter, DUP, *Heart Throbs of the West*, vol. 1, pp. 285-286.
9. John D. Rees, Kimball Young Collection.
10. Kate Carter, DUP, *Heart Throbs of the West*, vol. 1, pp. 293-294.
11. Orson Smith, Kimball Young Collection.
12. Kate Carter, DUP, *Our Pioneer Heritage*, vol. 12, pp. 86-87.
13. Agnes Melissa Stevens Wilson, Autobiography, 1962–(1963), Church Archives (paragraphing added).
14. Kate Carter, DUP, *Heart Throbs of the West*, vol. 1, p. 290.
15. *Ibid.*, pp. 281-282.
16. *Ibid.*, pp. 282-283 (paragraphing added).
17. Susan E. J. Martineau, *The Young Woman's Journal*, (The Young Ladies' Mutual Improvement Association of Zion, 1892), Special Collections, BYU, vol. 17, p. 542.
18. Kate Carter, DUP, *Heart Throbs of the West*, vol. 1, p. 287 (minor punctuation corrections).
19. Sketch of the life of Elizabeth Golightly Watt, (n.d.), Church Archives, p. 17.
20. Samuel Rose Parkinson, Diaries, 1876–1914, Church Archives (sequence and paragraphing altered).

21. Susa Young Gates Notebook, typescript, *Exponent*, 1898, Church Archives (minor spelling corrections, punctuation and paragraphing added).
22. Kate Carter, DUP, *Heart Throbs of the West*, vol. 1, pp. 290-291.
23. Kate Carter, DUP, *Our Pioneer Heritage*, vol. 5, pp. 211-212.

CHAPTER SIX

1. Agnes Melissa Stevens Wilson, Autobiography, 1962 – (1963), Church Archives.
2. Moses 1:39, *Pearl of Great Price*, (Church of Jesus Christ of Latter-day Saints, Salt Lake City, UT).
3. Joseph F. Smith, *Teachings of the Presidents of the Church*, (Church of Jesus Christ of Latter-day Saints, Salt Lake City, UT, 1998) p. 176.
4. *Journal of Discourses*, sermon by Joseph F. Smith, vol. 20, pp. 28-29 (paragraphing added).
5. *Hannah: An Autobiography by Hannah Simmons Gibb*, (Fisher House Publishers, Edmonton, Alberta, 1995), pp. 14-18.
6. *Journal of Discourses*, sermon by Orson Pratt, vol. 1, pp. 62-63 (paragraphing added).
7. Spencer W. Kimball, San Antonio Fireside, Dec. 3, 1977, pp. 11-12.
8. Joseph Fielding Smith, *Doctrines of Salvation*, 3 vols., ed. Bruce R. McConkie, (Bookcraft, Salt Lake City, UT, 1954-1956), vol. 2, p. 87.
9. Jane Charters Robinson Hindley, Journals 1855 – 1905, Church Archives.
10. Agnes Melissa Stevens Wilson, Autobiography, 1962 – (1963), Church Archives, p. 108.
11. B.H. Roberts, *Comprehensive History of the Church*, 6 vols., (Church of Jesus Christ of Latter-day Saints, Salt Lake City, UT, 1930), vol. 5, p. 295.

CHAPTER SEVEN

1. *LDS Biographical Encyclopedia*, ed. Andrew Jenson, 4 vols., (Andrew Jenson History Company, Salt Lake City, UT, 1901), vol. 1, p. 381.

2. Joseph Smith, *Teachings of the Prophet Joseph Smith*, compiled by Joseph Fielding Smith, (Deseret Book Co., Salt Lake City, UT, 1972), p. 357.
3. Joseph F. Smith, *Gospel Doctrine*, (Deseret Book Co., Salt Lake City, UT, 1971), pp. 93-94 (paragraphing added).
4. Helen Mar Whitney, "Why We Practice Plural Marriage", *Juvenile Instructor*, Salt Lake City, UT, 1884 (paragraphing added).
5. Bishop Victor L. Brown, "Our Youth: Modern Sons of Helaman", *Ensign*, Church of Jesus Christ of Latter-day Saints, Salt Lake City, UT, January 1974, p. 108 (paragraphing added).
6. Spencer W. Kimball, "Spoken From Their Hearts", *Ensign*, Church of Jesus Christ of Latter-day Saints, Salt Lake City, UT, November 1975.
7. Richard P. Lindsay, "Celebration of Families Conference", Worldwide Organization for Women, Salt Lake City, UT, March 13, 1999 (punctuation and paragraphing altered).
8. "The State of Our Unions", The National Marriage Project, (Rutgers, State University of New Jersey, 1999).
9. Barbara Ehrenreich, "Will Women Still Need Men?", *TIME Magazine*, February 21, 2000.
10. "Dutch Approve Gay Marriages", *Deseret News*, (Salt Lake City, UT), September 12-13, 2000.
11. Joseph F. Smith, *Teachings of the Presidents of the Church*, (Church of Jesus Christ of Latter-day Saints, Salt Lake City, UT, 1998), p. 174.
12. Dr. Laura Schlessinger, *Parenthood By Proxy*, (HarperCollins Publishers Inc., New York, NY, 2000), p. 246.
13. Gordon B. Hinckley, *Teachings of Gordon B. Hinckley*, (Deseret Book Co., Salt Lake City, UT, 1997), p. 408.
14. "Federal Dilution a Temptation for Faith-based Groups", *Deseret News,* (Salt Lake City, UT), February 4, 2001.
15. World Campaign, "Population Control", on-line, Internet, September 9, 2000, http://www.worldcampaign.com.
16. Editorial Comment, KRCL-91 FM, Salt Lake City, UT, 1999.
17. Bruce R. McConkie, *Mormon Doctrine*, (Bookcraft Inc., Salt Lake City, UT, 1970), p. 86 (paragraphing added).

18. Michael Secter, "The Baby Bust: A special report: Population Implosion Worries a Graying Europe", *The New York Times*, July 10, 1998.
19. The Alan Guttmacher Institute, "Sharing Responsibility: Women, Society and Abortion Worldwide", New York, 1999, pp. 21-22.
20. The Alan Guttmacher Institute, "Incidence of Abortion", Revised 2/2000.
21. The Population Research Institute, "China, the UNFPA, and 'Reproductive Rights'", (VA), vol. 2, no. 18, October 19, 2000.
22. *San Jose Mercury News*, "Experts Allege Infanticide in China", (CA), March 15, 2000.
23. BBC News, "China Steps Up 'One Child' Policy", (UK), September 25, 2000.
24. *Ibid*.
25. French Press Agency, AFP, (France), March 9, 2001.
26. The London Times, "The Baby Killers", (U.K.), March 12, 1997.
27. *Journal of Discourses*, sermon by Wilford Woodruff, vol. 23, p. 124.
28. Margaret Sanger, "Women and the New Race", (Brentano's, New York, 1920).
29. American Life League Inc., 2001.
30. Ohio Right to Life Society, "Abortion", on-line, Internet, August 20, 2001, http://www.ohiolife.org/life.asp.
31. American Life League Inc., 2001.
32. Nancy Naomi Alexander Tracy Autobiography, 1885, Special Collections, BYU, pp. 32-34.
33. Martin Luther King, Jr., Quotes On Freedom, on-line, Internet, November 2, 2000, http://www.angelfire.com/mn/rongstadliberty/Quotes.html.

CHAPTER EIGHT

1. Helen Mar Whitney, "Plural Marriage as Taught by the Prophet Joseph", *Juvenile Instructor*, Salt Lake City, UT, 1882.
2. Autobiography of Samuel Claridge, Church Archives.
3. Eliza R. Snow, *Woman's Exponent*, Church Archives, September 15, 1873, p. 62.

4. Helen Mar Whitney, "Why We Practice Plural Marriage", *Juvenile Instructor*, Salt Lake City, UT, 1884.
5. Emmeline Wells, *Woman's Exponent*, Church Archives, August 15, 1876, p. 44.
6. *The Diaries of Charles Ora Card, The Canadian Years, 1886-1903*, ed. Donald G. Godfrey and Brigham Y. Card, (University of Utah Press, Salt Lake City, UT, 1993), p. 37 (minor spelling and punctuation corrections).
7. Nancy Naomi Alexander Tracy Autobiography, 1885, Special Collections, BYU, pp. 30-31 (paragraphing added).
8. Gordon B. Hinckley, "Reach With a Rescuing Hand", *Ensign*, Church of Jesus Christ of Latter-day Saints, Salt Lake City, UT, November 1996, p. 85.

CHAPTER NINE

1. Joseph Smith, *Discourses of the Prophet Joseph Smith,* compiled by Alma P. Burton, (Deseret Book Co., Salt Lake City, UT, 1977), p. 70.
2. *Journal of Discourses*, sermon by Orson Hyde, vol. 2, p. 210.
3. *Journal of Discourses*, sermon by John Taylor, vol. 22, pp. 298-299 (paragraphing added)
4. Mark E. Petersen, *The Way of the Master*, (Bookcraft, Inc., Salt Lake City, UT, 1974), p. 43.
5. *Merriam-Webster's Collegiate Dictionary*, (Merriam-Webster, Inc., Springfield, MA), 10th ed.
6. Joseph Smith, *History of the Church of Jesus Christ of Latter-day Saints*, ed. B.H. Roberts, 7 vols., 2nd ed., rev. (Deseret Book Company, Salt Lake City, UT, 1971), vol. 4, p. 207.
7. Matthias F. Cowley, ed., *Wilford Woodruff, History of His Life and Labors*, (Bookcraft, Salt Lake City, UT, 1964), p. 542.
8. Jeffery L. Sheler, "The Mormon Moment", *U.S. News & World Report*, November 13, 2000, pp. 58-59.
9. Bruce R. McConkie, "The Coming Tests and Trials and Glory", *Ensign*, Church of Jesus Christ of Latter-day Saints, Salt Lake City, UT, May 1980, p. 71 (paragraphing added).

10. Gordon B. Hinckley, "What Are People Asking about Us?", *Ensign*, Church of Jesus Christ of Latter-day Saints, Salt Lake City, UT, November 1998, p. 70.
11. Irwin Altman & Joseph Ginat, *Polygamous Families in Contemporary Society*, (Cambridge University Press, Cambridge, NY, 1996), p. 40.
12. The Joseph Lee Robinson Journal, Special Collections, BYU, p. 9.
13. *Ibid.*, pp. 8-14, (minor word and punctuation changes, paragraphing added).
14. *Journal of Discourses*, sermon by Orson Pratt, vol. 17, p. 229.
15. Isaiah 4:1, *Holy Bible*, King James Version, Church of Jesus Christ of Latter-day Saints, footnote 1a.
16. *The Defense Monitor*, "The World at War", Center for Defense Information, Washington, DC, vol. 27, p. 4.
17. *Journal of Discourses*, sermon by George A. Smith, vol. 15, p. 27.
18. Charles Dickens, *A Tale of Two Cities*, (Trident Press International, Naples, FL, 2000), p. 1.
19. *Journal of Discourses*, sermon by John Taylor, vol. 23, p. 333.
20. Orson F. Whitney, Church of Jesus Christ of Latter-day Saints Conference Report, April 1921.

CHAPTER TEN

1. Helen Mar Whitney, "Why We Practice Plural Marriage", *Juvenile Instructor*, Salt Lake City, UT, 1884.
2. *Journal of Discourses*, sermon by George Q. Cannon, vol. 23, p. 278 (paragraphing added).
3. Edward W. Tullidge, *The Women of Mormondom*, (Tullidge & Crandall, New York, 1877), p. 295.
4. Joseph Smith, *Discourses of the Prophet Joseph Smith*, compiled by Alma P. Burton, (Deseret Book Co., Salt Lake City, UT, 1977), p. 70.
5. Gordon B. Hinckley, "Look to the Future", *Ensign*, Church of Jesus Christ of Latter-day Saints, Salt Lake City, UT, November 1997, p. 67.
6. Joseph Smith, *Documentary History of the Church*, 7 vols., (Deseret Book Co., Salt Lake City, UT, 1980), vol. 6, p. 184.

INDEX

~ A ~

Abortion 174-177
Adams, Sally 114
Adamson, Johannah 49
Afghanistan 175
Africa 196
Allred, Byron Harvey Sr. 120
Altman, Irwin 197
Amussen, Barbara Smith 41
Amussen, Carl Christian 41
Anderson, Amelia 88
Arizona 50, 67, 87
Arthur, Christopher J. 35
Asians 196
Atlanta, Georgia 201

~ B ~

Bailey, Charles R. 47
Ballard, Henry 59-60
Ballard, Margaret McNeil 59
Bangladesh 175
Barrowford, England 143
Baumann, Barbara 110
Bean, J. Will 80
Bean, Olive Smoot 80
Beck, Elizabeth Acord 35
Beck, Erastus 35
Benson, Ezra T. 199
Bentley, Joseph C. 46, 106
Blair, Elizabeth T. 132
Bleak, James G. 54
Bleak, Jane T. 54

Bott, Ada 82
Bott, John H. 82
Bowen, John 123
Brandley, Louis Orson 113
Brown, Bishop Victor L. 166
Brown, John 78
Bushman, Martin Benjamin 28

~ C ~

Cache Valley 48, 60-61
California 107
Call, Anson B. 78
Call, Julia Sarah Abegg 78
Callister, Helen M. 2
Canada 22-23, 187
Cannon, David 124
Cannon, George Q. 208
Card, Charles O. 187
Cardston, Alberta 187
Carling, Ellen A. 120
Carnegie Commission 201
Carpenter, Caroline Mariah 73, 128
Castle Garden 61
Cedar City 125
Celebration of Families Conference 167
Celestial 7-9, 15, 19, 21, 25, 33-34,
   38, 42, 53, 62, 68, 74, 80, 93, 105, 107,
   111, 152-153, 159-160, 188, 197, 203,
   210, 212, 233
Celestial Kingdom 105, 152-153
Chamberlain, Thomas 118
Chandler, Arabella Ann 143

China..174-175
Christensen, Anna 93
Christensen, Hannah 93
Christensen, Inger Anna.........................108
Christian Democratic Alliance.............169
Circleville, Utah 93
Claridge, Samuel......................20, 29, 180
Clayton, William....................7, 17, 44, 213
College Hall 103
Colonia Garcia 87
Congress...26
Connecticut 128
Constitution.....................................26, 232
Coombs, Fanny 54, 132
Coombs, Isaiah M. 53
Copenhagen..93, 98
Cottam, Catherine 94
Council Bluffs, Iowa 114
Covington, Chastie E. 120
Cowan, William & Mary B...................134

~ D ~

Denmark...98
DeWitt, Aaron 60
Diaz, Mexico..99
Dixie...55
Drammen, Norway...................................88
Durrant, Elizabeth Jane Ginger.............115
Durrant, John..115
Durrant, Joseph Smith...........................117
Dury, Julia Pamelia 35
Dutch 169

~ E ~

East, Wilmarth..25
Eden 3, 151
Egypt 196
Elijah 207
Elk Horn River 84

Endowment House..............49, 62, 86, 88, 93-94, 97-98, 126, 153
Ephraim, Utah 93
Erickson, Oluf..92
Europe......................18, 31, 85, 1731-174

~ F ~

Fackerell, Laura 120
Farmington, Utah 128
Farnsworth, Alonzo & Eda 86, 148
Foote, Warren..105
Fort Herriman, Utah..............................140
Franklin, Utah 59, 143

~ G ~

Gallacher, Mary Reiser 135
Gardner, Celestia Snow........................114
Gates, Susa Young.................................146
Georgia..201
German..137
Gibb, Hannah Simmons........................154
Gibb, Randall 156
Ginat, Joseph...197
Gloyd, Abigail...69
Gold Plates 23
Golightly, Elizabeth 52, 142
Grange, Samuel.......................................38
Great Salt Lake 24, 86
Green, John P. 60

~ H ~

Hagar...217, 222
Hale, Mary Ann......................................104
Hales, Vivian Parkinson Taylor 143
Hammond, John 132
Hammond, Sarah...................................132
Hardy, Charlotte Augusta........................54
Hardy, John Thomas 54
Hawkins, Susannah..................................49

Hawkins, Thomas 50-51
Hayward, Elizabeth 117
Heimberg, Karolina 110
Hinckley, Gordon B. 4, 170, 189, 196, 211, 243
Hindley, Jane C. R. 159
Holman, Harriett 104
Horne, Joseph 24
Horne, Mary Isabella 22, 24
Hoyt, Elinor A. 120
Hunt, Bishop John 63
Hunt, Ida 62-68
Huntington, Utah 37
Hurricane, Utah 125
Hyde, Mary Ann Price 41
Hyde, Orson 41-42, 191
Hyde, William 69

~ I ~

Idaho 143
Illinois 7, 213
India 175, 196, 198
Isaiah 201
Islam 196
Israel 196
Iverson, Jennie Cowan 134
Ivins, Caddie 147
Ivins, Julia M. 148

~ J ~

Jensen, Jens Iver 108
Jenson, Andrew 140
Jewish 196
Jianhua, Yuan 174
Johnson, Benjamin F. 20, 43, 103
Johnson, Joel Hills 140
Johnson, Ezekiel & Julia Hills ...140
Johnson, Miles Edgar 37
Johnson, Sarah Melissa Holman 104

~ K ~

Kay, Joseph 48
Kaysville, Utah 143
Kimball, Heber C. 30-34, 90-92
Kimball, Lucy Walker 14, 27, 90
Kimball, Spencer W. 158, 166
Kimball, Vilate 90
King, David 63, 65, 67
King, Martin Luther 177
Kirtland, Ohio 33, 43, 207
Kirtland Temple 207

~ L ~

Larsen, Oluf Christian 88
Lawrence, Sara 17
Layton, Utah 143
Layton, Alean Ellison 142
Leavitt, Adah Ann Waite 105
Leavitt, Mary Luella 101
Leavitt, Thomas Dudley 101
Lee, Harriet 98
Lee, Lester B. 212
Lehi 50, 69-70, 115
Leishman, Thomas 48
Leonard, William H. 39
Letter 7-8, 41, 52, 65-66, 70, 107
Levitt, Liddie 114
Lindsay, Richard P. 166
Liverpool, England 59
Logan, Utah 61, 128
London, England 175
Loverige, Phylinda 132
Luther, Martin 25, 177

~ M ~

Maggie 46, 106
Maine 97
Manifesto 36, 38, 121, 207
Mansfield, England 54
Marden, Belinda 68, 83-84

Marriage, Celestial 7-8, 15, 19, 21, 25, 34, 38, 42, 62, 68, 80, 93, 105, 107, 111, 152, 159-160, 203
Marriage, Patriarchal Order of.............194
Marriage, Rules of Plural...............25, 223
Martineau, Susan Ellen Johnson..........140
Maughan, Peter 47, 49
McArthur, Duncan 105
McConkie, Bruce R. 172, 195
Mears, Elizabeth......................................50
Mehring, Catharine E..............................59
Merrill, Marriner Wood...........................72
Mexico 36, 87, 96
Michigan 132
Missouri 31
Moroni, Angel 23
Morrison, Margaret Forquhar Cruickshank..129
Mortensen, Elizabeth Mears Hawkins...50
Mortensen, Ida Jane Pease 51
Mortensen, James 50-51
Moscow, Russia 196
Moses..................192, 201, 203, 213, 218
Musser, A. Milton 163

~ N ~

Naisbitt, Henry W....................................81
National Marriage Project....................168
Nauvoo, Illinois 7, 14, 30, 32, 42, 44, 72, 105-106, 114, 197, 209, 213
Neilsen, Sarah Ellis Farnsworth 86, 148
Nelson, Price 96
New York 59, 86, 132, 173
Nielsen, Anne Marie 98
Noah 192
Norway..88

~ O ~

Obery, Samuel 49

Obray, Sarah Ann 128
Ogden, Utah 60, 188
Ohio Right to Life................................176
Olsen, Emelia Christine 88
Olsen, Eva Jenson 140
Ostler, Rose Durrant.............................115

~ P ~

Pace, John Ezra 147
Pace, Phoebe Ann Covington...............147
Palestine 41
Paradise, Utah 128
Parkinson, Charlotte Smart 143
Parkinson, Samuel Rose.......................143
Parowan, Utah 53
Partridge, Emily 12, 17
Payne, Edward W. 98, 103
Payne, Lucy..103
Payne, Rozalia..98
Peking...196
Perry, Elizabeth 35
Petersen, Mark E...................................193
Phillips, Francis Ann 59
Pine Valley, Utah 114
Planned Parenthood..............................175
Polygamist 9, 29, 35, 78, 89-90, 103, 142, 145-146
Polygamous Families in Contemporary Society...197
Polygamy ....vii, 1, 3, 8-9, 35-36, 41, 46-47, 50, 56, 73, 78-79, 82-83, 96, 98-103, 106, 121, 129, 146, 165, 184, 186, 188, 193, 196, 198-200, 240
Population Control........................174-175
Pratt, Ann Agatha Walker 83
Pratt, Belinda Marden 68, 84
Pratt, Orson............24-25, 157, 201, 223
Pratt, Parley P. 68, 83-84
Pratt, Sarah......................................69-70

Preston, Idaho..........................145
Priesthood 21, 88, 92-93, 110, 145, 152-153, 182, 185, 187, 192-193, 200, 204, 214-215, 2175, 219, 221, 224
Proclamation 169, 241
Promise, Land of..................185
Provo, Utah 119
Pugsley, Phillip & Martha....................117
Putnam, Clarissa A................................99
Putnam, Savannah Clark..............99, 128

~ R ~

Ramus, Illinois 43, 140
Reeder, Leah Rees................126
Rees, John D. & Zillah M....................126
Reichen, Louise....................110
Reiser, Henry........................135
Reiser, Magdalena Schneider.............135
Richards, President Franklin D..............59
Roberts, B.H..........................21, 161
Robinson, Joseph Lee 197, 254
Rogers, Anna..........................114
Rolf, Matilda 121
Romania 175
Romel, Agnes........................135
Romney, Hannah Hood Hill..................94
Romney, Miles Park.............................94
Roundy, Elizabeth J. 25
Rowe vs. Wade......................176
Rowley Flats 39
Rowley, Hannah 39
Rowley, Samuel 38, 40
RUD438 176
Russia 173

~ S ~

Saigon....................................196
Sandwich Isles......................104
Sanger, Margaret 176

Santaquin, Utah.............45, 86, 104
Scarborough, Canada West 23
Schlessinger, Dr. Laura 170
Scotland..................................60
Scott, Madison M. Est...............8
Second Coming..................vii, 204
Sister-wives...................160, 186
Skinner, G. William 174
Smart, Charlotte 143
Smart, Maria..........................143
Smith, Bathsheba..............77, 111
Smith, Emma Hale.............9, 17, 220
Smith, George Albert 110, 202
Smith, Hyrum 8, 17, 44, 58, 200
Smith, Joseph F.............151-152, 163, 169
Smith, Joseph Fielding.........................158
Smith, Orson 73, 128
Smith, Patriarch John 60
Smith, Prophet Joseph 1, 7-8, 15, 18, 23, 30, 41, 89, 114, 122, 140, 152, 163, 165, 191-193, 200, 210-212, 213
Smoot, Abraham Owens 89
Smoot, Emily 80
Smoot, Margaret Thompson McMears..89
Snow, Eliza R. ...12, 18, 25, 128, 182, 209
Snow, Erastus 68
Snow, William 114
Snowflake, Arizona 50, 63-64, 67
St. George 46, 51, 57, 64, 115, 133
St. George Temple...........46, 64
St. Louis...................59, 134, 144
St. Paul...................................59
Stephenson, Elizabeth Ann 59
Stewart, Tommy 67
Stoner, Jane 134
Stout, Mary Viola Allred.....................120
Stucki, John S........................110
Supreme Court 176
Sweden..................................86

Sweetwater 48

~ T ~

Taylor, John 50, 94, 96, 141, 192, 194, 203
Taylor, Thomas 94
Teasdale, George 73
Telestial Kingdom 233
Temple, Kirtland 207
Temple, St. George 46, 64
Terrestrial Kingdom 233
Terry, Charles & Sarah H. 132-133
Tietjen, August & Eda............................86
Tracy, Nancy Naomi Alexander...177, 188

~ U ~

Udall, David King......................63, 65, 67
Udall, Ida Hunt.......................................67

~ V ~

Vietnam 175

~ W ~

Walker War......................................45, 104
Washington, D.C. 25
Watson, Margaret Smith 128
Watt, Elizabeth Golightly....................142
Watt, George D. 52, 142
Webb, Eva C. 124
Wells, Emmeline 25, 186
Wellsville, Utah......................................49
Weslton, Martha 28
White, Margaret Rees 126
Whitney, Elizabeth 246
Whitney, Elizabeth Ann 42
Whitney, Helen Mar.......74, 107, 165,179, 183, 207
Whitney, Horace K...............................107
Whitney, Orson F. 204
Wilson, Agnes Melissa Stevens ...131, 151
Wilson, Emeline 133
Wilson, Guy C..131
Wines, Maria 114
Winter Quarters.....................................72
Wood, Emma Louise Elliker................108
Wood, Sam 108
Woodruff................22, 29, 64, 97-98, 107, 175, 194-195, 207
Woodruff, Abraham Owen 22
Woodruff, Phoebe 107
Woodruff, Wilford.................29, 107, 175, 194-195, 207
Woodsmansee, Gladys 46
Woolley, Edwin Dilworth 57
Woolley, John Mills 57
Woolley, Mary E. 120
Woolley, Samuel Amos 57
Wright, Mary Ellen 128

~ Y ~

Young, Brigham............21, 24, 26, 28, 31, 55-57, 68, 72, 78, 135, 146
Young, Lucy Bigelow 146
Young, Seymore B. 37